GREAT HISTORIC DISASTERS

THE
TRIANGLE SHIRTWAIST FACTORY FIRE

GREAT HISTORIC DISASTERS

GREAT HISTORIC DISASTERS

THE
TRIANGLE SHIRTWAIST
FACTORY FIRE

BRENDA LANGE

CHELSEA HOUSE
PUBLISHERS

An imprint of Infobase Publishing

THE TRIANGLE SHIRTWAIST FACTORY FIRE

Chelsea House
An imprint of Infobase Publishing
132 West 31st Street
New York, NY 10001

Library of Congress Cataloging-in-Publication Data
Lange, Brenda.
The Triangle Shirtwaist Factory fire/Brenda Lange.
   p.   cm.—(Great historic disasters)
Includes bibliographical references and index.
ISBN: 978-0-7910-9641-3 (hardcover)
1. Triangle Shirtwaist Company—Fire, 1911—Juvenile literature. 2. New York (N.Y.)—History—1898-1951—Juvenile literature. 3. Clothing factories—New York (State)—New York—Safety measures—History—20th century—Juvenile literature. 4. Labor laws and legislation—New York (State)—New York—History—20th century—Juvenile literature. I. Title.
F128.5.L237 2008
974.7'041—dc22   2007037042

Chelsea House books are available at special discounts when purchased in bulk quantities for businesses, associations, institutions, or sales promotions. Please call our Special Sales Department in New York at (212) 967-8800 or (800) 322-8755.

You can find Chelsea House on the World Wide Web
at http://www.chelseahouse.com

Text design by Annie O'Donnell
Cover design by Ben Peterson

Printed in the United States of America

Bang KT 10 9 8 7 6 5 4 3 2 1

This book is printed on acid-free paper.

All links and Web addresses were checked and verified to be correct at the time of publication. Because of the dynamic nature of the Web, some addresses and links may have changed since publication and may no longer be valid.

Contents

Introduction:
Tragedy at the Factory

The date was Saturday, March 25, 1911. The warm, spring day began just like any other workday for hundreds of thousands of working-class people in New York City. But it would end in tragedy for 146 victims of one of the city's worst workplace disasters and their families. And it would set the wheels in motion for radical workplace reforms.

The long day was winding down, and the sky was beginning to darken as twilight descended on the city. It was the end of a normal 60- to 70-hour workweek—Monday through Saturday—for employees of the Triangle Shirtwaist Factory. Most were looking forward to a day of rest with their families. Those who remained that afternoon were mainly women, as the male employees—who performed the more physically challenging jobs of cutting material—had finished work for the day. The seamstresses and helpers had stayed to wrap up their final projects for the week and pack away supplies.

Suddenly, at about 4:30 P.M., they heard what sounded like an explosion, and shouts arose from the Asch Building at Washington Place and Green Street, next to Washington Square Park. The top three floors of this 10-story tenement building—where the Triangle Factory was located—were on fire.

Although some people later had theories about the origin of the fire, no one knows exactly what started it. Perhaps it was a cigarette or match carelessly tossed into a pile of rags, or perhaps the cause was a malfunctioning sewing machine. Flammable materials were everywhere, and it would not have taken much for a fire to start and spread.

The eighth, ninth, and tenth floors had dozens of sewing machines that workers used to churn out shirtwaists, a popular form of women's clothing in the early twentieth century. Rented by the Triangle Shirtwaist Company, the factory was just one of hundreds such tenement factories throughout New York City. Shops like this one were known as sweatshops, as much for their hot, airless conditions as for the amount of hard work put in there. Most of the employees were poor immigrants with no training or education and few options for better work. Constructing shirtwaists became a way of life for thousands.

A shirtwaist was a blouse with puffy sleeves and a collar. Similar to a man's button-down dress shirt, shirtwaists came in many different styles but were always tailored at the waist to make them more flattering to a woman's figure. They usually were worn with long, dark skirts. Stitching them together required the work of many people—often teenage girls and sometimes girls as young as 10 or 11 who were sent to work to help feed their families. About 500 workers were employed by Triangle. Although there were some men, Triangle employees were mostly older teen girls and women in their twenties.

Several fire departments responded quickly to the call, but the fire spread rapidly, burning scraps of cloth and debris, tables, and baskets. There were no sprinklers. The fire began on the eighth floor, but most workers there were able to escape by using the stairs to the roof, where they then scrambled to neighboring roofs and safety. Many workers became trapped on the ninth floor, unable to get into the narrow stairwell because the access door was locked and the elevator broken. An administrative assistant called in the alarm and alerted the workers on the tenth floor, but no one knows why the warning phone call to the ninth floor was delayed by several precious minutes.

A large crowd soon gathered in the streets below. Necks craned to watch as girls stood in the open windows, flames licking at their long skirts. Frantic friends and relatives ran through the crowd, inquiring after their loved ones. Relief spread as firefighters arrived at the scene with 35 trucks and other equipment. Several new motorized fire trucks arrived with long ladders. But it was already too late for a few girls who had fallen or jumped from the windows.

Quickly, the firemen raised the ladders toward the waiting workers. Groans of disbelief and disappointment rose from the crowd as the fully extended ladders bounced uselessly against the side of the building, at least a floor below the trapped workers. In desperation, some of the girls began trying to climb out of the building. Others jumped for the ladder but missed and fell to the sidewalk below. Firemen held out safety nets, but even one with a steel frame

The Triangle Shirtwaist Factory's inadequate fire escape *(above)* melted from the heat of the fire and collapsed under the weight of the girls who were trying to flee the inferno.

could not support the combined weight of the girls who jumped into them. The fabric ripped, and they also landed on the sidewalk.

The scene was nightmarish as darkness began to fall and heavy smoke billowed from the building. Ash fell onto those watching, and the flames were finally subdued. It did not take long for the firemen to extinguish the fire once they could get inside and drag their heavy hoses up with them, but that is when the true nightmare began for families of the trapped workers.

In all, 146 were killed either by flame, smoke, or falls from windows. A makeshift morgue was set up on the Twenty-Sixth Street Pier on the East River, and horse-drawn carriages carried the bodies away to await identification. It took nearly a week for all the bodies to be claimed; seven never were identified.

How did such a tragedy happen? This was not the first time a massive workplace accident had claimed many lives in New York and in the country as a whole, and it would not be the last. But this terrible event shocked everyone who heard about it. The tragic loss of life was just one part of the story. The fact that the fire, or at least the high number of deaths, could have been prevented was another. Almost immediately, demand began for Triangle's owners to be put on trial. The *New York Evening Journal* pictured a dead worker lying on the pavement with a caption reading, "Is anyone to be punished for this?"

This harrowing event at the Triangle Factory was a turning point in the campaign for workers' rights and workplace safety. There had been efforts for years to provide better conditions for factory workers, but it took a massive loss of life to gain widespread recognition for the plight of the working poor in the United States.

1

Immigration and Life on the Lower East Side

For many people in Europe during the nineteenth century, America was seen as a safe haven—a place where they would be able to live comfortably, without government or religious harassment. They believed in tales of valuable opportunities for work and a better life around every corner. So convincing were these stories, that immigrants flooded the shores of the United States by the millions. Unfortunately, many of them merely exchanged the harsh existence of the Old World for the same, or sometimes worse, life in the new. Dreams of riches rarely materialized. But these new Americans made the most of their situations by settling in areas with others from their country, setting up homes and businesses, and educating their children so they could have better lives.

WHO CAME AND WHY

During the early part of the 1800s, most immigrants to the United States came from England and Germany. New residents crossed the Atlantic at the rate of about 60,000 each year. Between 1830 and 1860, that rate shot up to nearly 5

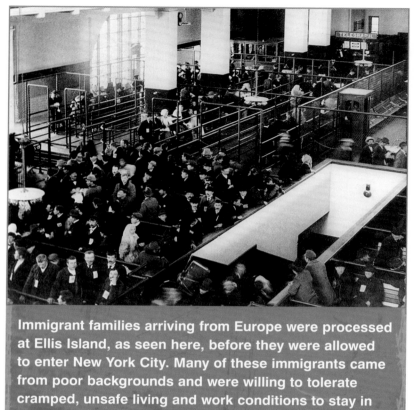

Immigrant families arriving from Europe were processed at Ellis Island, as seen here, before they were allowed to enter New York City. Many of these immigrants came from poor backgrounds and were willing to tolerate cramped, unsafe living and work conditions to stay in the United States.

million. They came for different reasons: Irish immigrants fleeing the Potato Famine of the 1840s were by far the largest group to come in the mid-1800s. Poor harvests for many years in Germany also prompted a high number of immigrants from that country. More than one million Swedes emigrated in the second half of the nineteenth century, reducing that country's population by one-fourth! Swedes came for a variety of reasons, including lack of available land, forced military service, and religious persecution in their homeland. For the most part, these immigrants continued west to Minnesota and the Dakotas by a combination of riverboat and railroad. The American Civil War kept many would-be settlers away, but immigration numbers were back up to prewar levels by 1880.

Nearly 24 million people entered the United States between 1881 and 1920; they were mainly from countries in southern and eastern Europe, including Russia, Poland, Greece, and Italy. The biggest group came between 1905 and 1914, when more than one million made the trip each year. Most of these new immigrants came to escape hunger and poverty caused by the rapid growth of industrialization across Europe. Millions there had moved from rural areas into the cities looking for work and hoped to make better lives for their families. Unfortunately, that often was not the case, and these immigrants found themselves in similar situations once they settled in the United States. Most of these immigrants were farmworkers; only about 14 percent brought a skill with them that could translate into a nonagricultural job in America. Others, such as Jews from Russia and eastern Europe, came to escape religious persecution.

Once they arrived, some of these travelers planned to continue their journey westward, and quite a few made it to the Midwest. But many stayed in the cities along the East Coast, either because they did not have any money to travel farther or because they knew people already living there. Parts of Boston, Philadelphia, and New York soon became severely overcrowded. Thousands of immigrants ended up settling in neighborhoods already established by countrymen who had come before them. These new immigrants were different from America's earlier groups of immigrants, and they often did not fit in with those already living there. They did not speak English, for one thing, and they often were illiterate even in their native tongue. There were frequent problems with the police because so many new immigrants were suspicious of authority; all too often in their homelands, those who had held authority had also abused it.

The immigrants moving into these cultural communities found comfort among others who spoke the same language, enjoyed the same foods, and shared the same cultural history. Often these tight-knit communities had specialty food stores and restaurants, churches or synagogues, and even newspapers in their own languages. Very often, immigrants from nearby

Social Darwinism

The theory of Social Darwinism was discussed among the rich and powerful, who took it as fact. They believed that those who had money and therefore, power, were meant to live that way because they were in some way stronger than the poor and powerless. The rich believed this was the way of the world, a fact that could not be changed. They pointed to Charles Darwin's theories of evolution and natural selection to support their beliefs that they were better than the poor. Andrew Carnegie, a prominent businessman and philanthropist, said, "We accept and welcome, as conditions to which we must accommodate ourselves, great inequality of wealth and environment, the concentration of business, industrial and commercial, in the hands of the few, as being not only beneficial, but essential for the future of the race." The poor working class was told to "submit cheerfully to authority and learn self-control."

Philip S. Foner, *The Policies and Practices of the American Federation of Labor 1900–1909* (New York: International Publishers, 1964), p. 26

villages in the old country settled in adjacent apartments in New York, effectively transplanting the old country to the United States. It was hard for the immigrants to be so far away from their homeland. Many had left loved ones behind, including aging parents, with the full knowledge they might never see them again.

Traveling to the United States was difficult for these immigrants, who often endured a long, frightening journey across the Atlantic Ocean by ship. Large steamer ships carrying 1,000 or more passengers made the trip in two or three weeks. Often families were crammed together below deck in dank conditions. Many became seasick or suffered other ailments on board the ship. Lice and dysentery made many travelers uncomfortable. Those ships that arrived in New York harbor stopped at Ellis Island, where millions of immigrants were processed for entry into the country between 1892 and 1924, with thousands going through medical exams each day. About 1,000 were not allowed entry every month for a variety of medical reasons, included tuberculosis, epilepsy, wheezing, or mental disorders. Sometimes a sick person was put back on a ship and sent home.

WHERE DID THEY LIVE?

According to staff at the Lower East Side Tenement Museum in New York, the first tenement was built in 1833 on Water Street in lower Manhattan. At that time, residences were normally built for single families. But enterprising businessmen realized the need for inexpensive, multiple-family dwellings as immigrants continued to come to America throughout the mid-1800s. By packing many families into small spaces intended for one family, these landlords could make a lot of money. Those who rented these apartments in tenements did so because it was all they could afford. By the mid-1860s, 800,000 people called New York City home. Of that number, more than 60 percent lived in tenements.

Tenement buildings were usually four to six stories high and constructed of brick. Their facades were dirty from the constantly swirling dust raised by horse-drawn carriages. It was noisy outside from the calls of pushcart peddlers and children at play, and it was also noisy inside from the sheer number of people living in a confined area. Privacy was nonexistent. The first floor and basement levels often contained shops such as bakeries, shoemakers, and laundries. Gas lines were installed in many buildings around 1900, allowing for gas lamps and cooking. When legislation passed ordering more light and access to better air, landlords sometimes cut windows in walls separating inner rooms from those around the outside of the building, letting in indirect sunlight.

Although living in cramped, dark, and somewhat primitive conditions, the inhabitants of these tenements did their best to maintain their dignity and sense of purpose. Women regularly swept the steps and washed down walls, which were often covered with inexpensive wallpaper held up by a paste made from flour and water. They hung family portraits or ripped ads from newspapers or pictures from calendars to decorate their walls. Family heirlooms might have been transported to America, although many of these immigrants had to sell precious belongings just to pay passage for themselves and family and have a little money to get settled once they arrived. For the most part, they did the best with what they had.

In the Lower East Side Tenement Museum at 97 Orchard Street in Manhattan, modern-day visitors can tour seven apartments that were inhabited from the late 1800s through 1920. According to the museum's Web site (www.tenement.org), in 1914 about 40 percent of all New Yorkers had been born in another country, and 97 Orchard Street was home to about 7,000 of those immigrants over the years. They came from more than 20 countries between the years of 1863 and 1935. The guided tours include historical information about the different

Tenement buildings were the only kind of housing poor immigrant families could afford in New York City. To maximize their profits, builders omitted gas and water amenities, so most families did not have heat or running water. Many tenements featured an outhouse in the back *(above)*. Laws requiring safer, more comfortable conditions were rarely enforced.

families that lived there, where they came from, and details about their experiences. These apartments have been decorated based on photographs from that era and according to the memories of the descendants of the original inhabitants.

These old photos prove that the new Americans had the taste and inclination to decorate their homes to make them as comfortable as they could. At a mere 300 to 400 square feet, there is no doubt the places were cramped—especially because families typically had five or more children. By 1900, the Lower East Side was home to 700 people per acre.

By 1911, most American cities had large Jewish neighborhoods, but New York's was the largest by far. Synagogues, libraries, stores, and mutual aid societies were established by the first Jewish settlers. Being so immersed in familiar culture helped the new settlers immeasurably as they adjusted to life in their new country.

LIVING CONDITIONS IN THE CITIES

Life was not easy for these immigrants. Many came to America with job skills that were useless in a city. For example, many new settlers had been farmers in their old countries, but there was little need for agricultural workers on the streets of Manhattan. Those who had grown up on farms with vast expanses of open countryside around them had big adjustments to make, living in cramped, dirty, city conditions.

In fact, American farmers were moving to the cities too. As industrialization grew across America, jobs in the cities were plentiful, and there was enormous demand for unskilled and semiskilled laborers to fill positions. Often, different ethnic groups came to be lumped into different work categories: Italians ended up working in road and building construction; Slavs worked in coal mines and the steel industry; and Jews, who came mostly from Russia and eastern Europe, often had skills that could translate into the light industry that was growing in various U.S. cities. These Jewish immigrants worked in the clothing, woodworking, and tobacco industries, but especially in the garment trade in New York City.

The streets of the Lower East Side of New York—defined as the area of Manhattan bounded by Fourteenth Street on the north, Catherine Street on the south, Broadway on the west, and the East River on the east—were teeming with people. People were always outside, whenever possible, even in cold weather, probably to escape their tiny apartments. There were few phones and, of course, no Internet, so people socialized face to face. These neighborhoods were close knit, and everyone knew everyone else—in many cases, they were even related. Horse-drawn carriages competed for street space with pushcart peddlers who sold everything from fruit and vegetables to books and trinkets.

According to Philip S. Foner in his book *The Policies and Practices of the American Federation of Labor 1900–1909*, living conditions in this neighborhood could be pretty grim. He cites statistics claiming that one block surveyed in that section of the city included 39 apartment buildings, with 605 separate apartments that had 2,871 people living in them. Only 40 apartments had water, and there were no indoor bathrooms. A small outhouse in the alleyway might serve all these people.

Often these homes also were makeshift factories. Immigrants supplemented their meager wages by bringing work home. This enabled the women to care for very small children while still earning some money for the family. This also allowed the whole family to participate. Sewing was a common type of "homework," but so, too, was cigar wrapping and packaging of various items. An investigation made by the National Child Labor Committee in New York State in 1912 found that, out of 181 families surveyed, 251 children under age 16 were working. Even four-year-olds were found working in some homes, making paper flowers for sale on the street. Sometimes all this extra work, with the whole family chipping in, might earn only five dollars a week. But those five dollars might get a family just enough milk, bread, or meat to eat a little better for another week.

The tall apartment buildings separated by narrow alleyways were their homes. All too often, several generations lived within two or three rooms of one apartment. A family considered itself lucky if its apartment was along the outside of the building, because then at least there was a window to

Many immigrants lacked useful skills and were forced to take low-paying jobs in factories. Women often supplemented their husbands' income with work they could do at home while watching the children, many of whom helped. *Above*, in a photograph from 1912, the females of the Mortaria family make flower wreaths until late in the evening.

open for light and air. If an apartment was within the inner core of the building, it was always dark, and the air was heavy and unhealthy, with ventilation coming only from narrow air-shafts. It was common to find three children sharing a bed in the same room as their parents.

Sometimes there was only one kitchen for two or three apartments. Sounds of children playing, parents arguing, and of daily family life filled the halls along with smells of cooking. Some apartments did not have ovens, and so the women prepared meals such as stews or bread and then took them to a local bakery to be baked or cooked. The owner of the bakery gave the women tickets for their pots of stew or loaves of bread, and then the women returned at a set time, with their tickets, to pick up the finished product.

Sanitation was poor or nonexistent. If there was indoor plumbing, the toilet would be located in a small room in the hallway, and even if there was a water source inside the building, the water coming out of the pipes was usually cold. More often than not, everyone in the tenement shared one or two outdoor toilets in a small outhouse behind the building. Electrical and fire safety codes were often broken or completely ignored.

Some landlords did not feel that they needed to keep their buildings in good condition because there was never a shortage of people looking for apartments in which to live.

WOMEN'S LIVES

Women's lives were very different in the early 1900s than they are today. A woman often worked only until she was married, and then she left her job to take care of her house, husband, and children. Women were more submissive, and they were raised to do what they were told, especially by men. First they had to obey their fathers and, later, their husbands. Women who were left alone—often with children to support—whether through death or divorce, had to struggle to survive. If a woman could sew—and most could—she could make enough to pay rent, buy food, and send her children to school. Women's fashions were sometimes very ornate and complicated, so any woman who was handy with a sewing machine and needle and thread could usually make a living.

Speaking up did not come easily for most women. When they did try to advocate for themselves and other women, they often were ridiculed, and their efforts got nowhere. Women knew that if they could vote, they would have more of a voice in determining how their lives would be led, but they still did not have the right to vote in 1911. But as more and more women entered the workforce, the suffragist movement gained in popularity. Suffragettes were advocates who spoke out for the right of women to vote. Although certain states and territories, such as Wyoming, Washington, and California, granted women the right to vote sooner, it took the passage of the Nineteenth Amendment in 1920 before all American women gained that right.

Many of these suffragettes were women who did not have to work, whose husbands had good jobs and positions of authority and power in the social structure of the city. Eventually, working women joined the ranks of the suffragettes, sometimes through unions that were formed at work. Increasing numbers of women began to realize that workplace conditions, as well as poor social conditions for women in general, were unlikely to improve without some sort of government representation. They realized that if they had the right to vote for men who cared about their interests, they might actually have a voice in the conditions under which they worked and lived. Without the right to vote, however, they had little power to make social changes for themselves and their daughters.

It was not until after World War I that a special department was set up by the U.S. Congress to help with women's issues in the workplace. This Women's Bureau was established after much lobbying by unions and politicians, with the mission to improve working conditions and the welfare of working women and to advance women's opportunities in the workplace. Unfortunately, these improvements came too late for the young female employees of the Triangle Factory.

2 Industry in America

Industry had been growing in the United States for more than a century by the time of the Triangle Factory fire. In fact, the first industry in the country was a glass-making "factory" in the colony at Jamestown, which was settled in 1607. But it was different from the factories most people know today. Several glassblowers worked in a large room on individual projects. Factories began using assembly lines during the Industrial Revolution. The first assembly-line textile factory was built in 1813 in Waltham, Massachusetts, and several others were built in Lowell, Massachusetts, in 1824. These factories were the first in the world to bring in cotton and ship out cloth, doing all the manufacturing under one roof. This was a new concept for Americans, and the procedures followed in Massachusetts were used as models for other factories.

Today, people are familiar with the idea of assembly line manufacturing, where one machine or person produces, assembles, or inspects only the materials needed for the next machine or person down the line, and so on, until the finished product emerges at the end. This type of manufacturing is used for all types of products, from cars to candy bars. And although it seems easy, it can be quite complicated to ensure that there is enough raw material at the beginning of the process and that the machines and workers do their jobs at just the right time so that the finished product ends up the way it is supposed to.

EARLY FACTORIES

Before the mills at Waltham and Lowell were built, there were "accidental" factories. For example, a lumberman might have a sawmill in which he cut trees into planks. The power to run the mill was most likely provided by water. Since the power was already being provided, the mill owner might add a couple of other machines—in the case of cloth production, a spinning mill or loom—which also needed water power to run. Early factories that ground grain into flour were started the same way. But the first textile factories in Massachusetts were the result of businessmen intentionally looking for new ways to invest their money. In Lowell, for example, two partners built the first factory where two rivers converged and a high waterfall provided energy. These partners, Patrick Jackson and Nathan Appleton, wanted their factory to have high standards, including good working conditions for their employees.

Bringing workers and machines together in one place also helped the owners and managers of these industries keep a close eye on their employees and ensure they did a full day's work. This constant supervision sometimes created a better and more uniform finished product. And once the work became fully mechanized, it was impossible to complete the work at home anyway. The factories in Lowell depended on a workforce of young—usually teenage—women. These women were housed in company-owned boardinghouses, similar to college dormitories, and supervised closely by older women who made sure the girls followed strict rules. Although these young workers were not slaves, their pay was meager, and they sometimes called themselves "wage slaves," according to Smithsonian.org. Before the rise of organized unions that

Popularized by automaker Henry Ford, assembly lines revolutionized manufacturing. The advent of the assembly line made it possible for factories to produce large quantities of products quickly. *Above*, men fill, weigh, and sew bags of sugar at a C&H Sugar factory.

lobbied for higher pay and shorter hours, disgruntled workers might stage a slowdown, where they did their jobs very slowly. Or they might quit in the middle of the day, leaving their employer with no one to finish a job. These tactics were more effective once individuals began to organize and stage slowdowns or walkouts as a group.

Within 15 years, the Merrimack Manufacturing Company, established by Jackson and Appleton in Lowell, had attracted thousands of workers to what was once a small town. A steady stream of potential factory workers was created both by country folk relocating to the city and by recently arrived Europeans. By 1836, the population was at 17,000, with 7,500 workers at eight mills in the area. Even though they worked 12-hour days, six days a week, they still found time to participate in the social life of the town, attending churches, concerts, and even publishing the *Lowell Offering*, a literary magazine, and later, the *Voice of Industry*, a newspaper that brought attention to negative working conditions.

Dissatisfied workers staged strikes in 1853 and were successful in getting the workday reduced to 11 hours from 13. And in 1912, a strike was successful in getting an increase in pay. It is surprising that it took so long for conditions to improve, but just as in the bigger cities, Lowell had its share of poor, unskilled immigrants willing to work for wages that were unacceptable to the former factory employees: girls from rural America. Not only were these new workers willing to work for less pay, but they also worked longer hours without grumbling, at least at first. But as in the bigger cities, workers eventually organized, taking their concerns and problems to management, realizing that they had more power to make changes in their work environment when they spoke up as a group rather than as individuals. When working conditions, including pay, hours, and safety concerns, did not advance along with the technological advances happening around the country, this type of group empowerment, or unionization, took hold.

As early as the Revolutionary War era, disgruntled workers realized they had to band together in order to get treated more fairly by employers. Early unions were formed in an attempt to bring improvements to unsafe jobs and to regulate hours and wages. Trade unions were formed by groups of men who were skilled in the same type of craft or trade. Some of the earliest trades to try unionizing were shoemakers in Philadelphia, carpenters in Boston, and printers in New York, all in the 1790s. About 30 years later, the first industrial unions formed;

Landsmanshaftn

Immigrants tended to settle in communities with men and women from the same country. These communities included areas of New York City such as Little Italy or Chinatown. The Lower East Side of New York was heavily settled by Jews from all over Europe. When they arrived in New York, one of the first things many of the new Jewish immigrants did was join a *landsmanshaftn*.

A landsmanshaftn was a Jewish benefit society of immigrants who came from the same region or town. The official names of these groups might be Independent Benevolent Society or Young Men's Society, along with the name of the village or area. Some were the First Independent Gostyniner Benevolent Society and the Shater Progressive Benevolent Association.

There were thousands of landsmanshaftn in New York in the early 1900s. They provided members with places to socialize and get advice on economic, social, and cultural problems. It must have been comforting to know there was a place to go where there would be people who believed as you did, spoke the same language, and had a similar background.

In addition, these societies often provided financial assistance to help new arrivals with expenses around the birth of a baby, a funeral, or medical costs. The landsmanshaftn were popular for all these reasons. For a small annual fee, around five dollars per member, the benefit societies helped the transition to a new life. They provided a sense of continuity and community, with members attending the same synagogue, working and living in the same places, and marrying within their culture. It was an organized way that earlier immigrants could help their countrymen adjust to their new lives.

they were made up of people who worked in the same type of industry, such as the steel industry, regardless of the job they held within that industry.

IMMIGRANTS AND THEIR JOBS IN NEW YORK CITY

Jobs that were available for unskilled workers were found mainly in the garment industry. Very often, these factories occupied an entire floor or more within a tenement building. The city of New York tried to regulate this industry, but many factories were unlicensed or unregistered. Unscrupulous

W.D. Haywood *(center)*, a union activist and organizer, leads a strike parade in Lowell, Massachusetts, in this photo. Factories in this small town employed mostly young women, who were often exploited by their employers and overseers. The first strikes occurred when businesses began to reduce wages.

owners crammed dozens of workers into small rooms with little or no ventilation—there was no heat in the freezing winter months and, obviously, no air-conditioning in the sweltering summer months. The lighting was poor, and workers' eyesight suffered. Men and women put in long hours at work, sometimes 12 or 14 hours a day, six or even seven days a week. There were no contracts telling the owners they had to let the workers in at 9 A.M. and out at 5 P.M., with an hour off for lunch and two 15-minute breaks. The owners made their own rules, which were rarely in favor of the employees. Pay was also very poor. In 1910, a man in the garment industry might make around $20 a week, while a woman would earn considerably less. These were all reasons these types of workplaces came to be known as sweatshops.

DANGEROUSLY LOW WAGES

Some factory owners, including the owners of the Triangle Company, used sneaky tactics to keep wages low. Instead of hiring seamstresses at a higher pay rate, they hired young girls, maybe 12 or 13 years old, as messengers within the factories and promoted them. At first these helpers were paid less than four dollars a week; soon, they could be promoted to button sewers for about one dollar more. Within a couple of years, the teenagers could become sewing machine operators for as little as a three-dollar raise.

Factory owners also actively recruited new immigrants, many of whom were already skilled seamstresses. They could be had for as little as six dollars a week, gradually earning top pay of about $12. Paying workers per piece encouraged them to get faster at their work, but once they were fast enough to make some real money, the owners would change their rate of pay to a straight salary. It was an unfair system, but the young women, especially newcomers to the United States, had few options. In 1905, an annual salary of $800 was considered the minimum necessary for a family of four. The average salary a factory worker could make was nearly half that, or about only $400 a year.

All too often, the factory buildings were unsafe. Windows did not always open, and some had bars across them. Fire escapes, when buildings had them, were more often than not old, rusty, and weak. Or they sometimes did not even reach the ground, such as the one at the Triangle Company. Even though automatic sprinkler systems had been developed in the late 1800s, these tenement factories usually did not have such systems in place, in part because the law did not yet require them. Employers routinely locked doors leading to stairs, which was against city regulations, in order to keep their employees inside so they did not "waste time" going to the bathroom too often. Doors also were locked so employees could not sneak out at quitting time with stolen merchandise hidden in their pockets or purses. It was common practice for factory managers to have their workers walk out, single file, with pocketbooks open for inspection.

PUTTING CHILDREN TO WORK

Perhaps the worst infraction committed by these factory owners and managers was the hiring of young children. Child labor in many industries, including mining, farming, and the garment trade, was legal in 1900—indeed, about 250,000 children under age 15 worked legally. But by 1911, child-labor reform laws had been passed nationally. Even so, many of these immigrant families could barely support themselves, even with both parents and older teens working. Families then were large, and everyone who could help was put to work. In order to have enough to eat, children as young as seven could be sent out to work. In the garment industry, they could be found sorting buttons, winding yarn or thread, or running errands for adults. It was bad enough that these youngsters were working days that might be 10 hours long. But, in addition, they received little or no schooling while they were working, meaning they might never be able to improve their lives through education. Inspectors who occasionally visited these factories might not find these young children, because if they were seen, the factory owners would be fined or get in trouble with the city. If they were licensed, they could lose their license. So the factory managers hid these illegal, young workers in baskets of material, or behind a door, or anywhere that they could remain unseen until the coast was clear.

WOMEN IN THE WORKPLACE

Businesses such as the Triangle Company usually employed many young women and children. Owners did not hire many men because male factory workers performed higher-paying jobs. For example, men did jobs that were more difficult and required more strength to perform, such as material cutting.

It was commonplace for girls to leave school by the eighth grade, if they even were allowed to attend that long, and to go to work to help support their families. Any money for education was spent on the boys in the family, since young women most often married and left the workforce to raise their children.

By 1911, about 7.5 million American women worked outside the home. Many women who lived in cities worked as seamstresses either at home or in factories. Women generally performed what was known as piecework. This simply meant they would work on specific pieces of a garment. For example, they might sew 10 buttons on the front of 10 shirts in a day. Or they might be responsible for hemming skirts or adding collars to blouses. Very often, women took this work home, piling dozens of clothing pieces in a large basket and lugging it to their apartments. Doing this type of homework allowed these women to care for infants while they contributed to the household's finances. Usually, the kitchen table turned into a mini factory during the day, where garments were assembled or other items were put together. Women

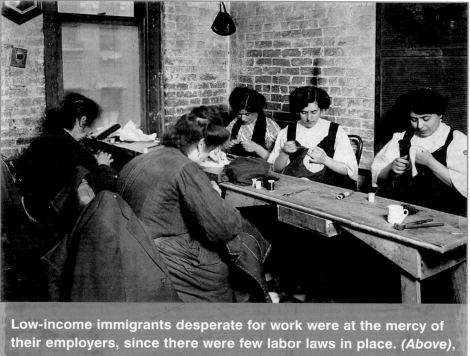

Low-income immigrants desperate for work were at the mercy of their employers, since there were few labor laws in place. *(Above)*, women sew garments in a room with no ventilation. Many of these sweatshops were built as shoddily as the tenement buildings in which the workers lived, without indoor plumbing, ventilation, light, or fire safety.

taught their daughters to sew at an early age and, by doing so, passed skills down through the generations.

Some women were fortunate to have skills that enabled them to earn more money—by teaching or nursing, for example. But most women worked at jobs that required no real training. Some women took in laundry, and others went to work as domestics, or servants, in the homes of others. Domestics cared for children, did laundry and housework, and cooked for the families of their wealthy employers. Women always had been second-class citizens to their husbands or fathers. If a woman was a widow with children to support, or if her husband was disabled, she had no choice but to join the workforce, where she always feared losing her job. Even single young women often were the sole support for their parents and siblings. In the case of the Triangle Company, 37 of the girls who died left behind relatives in Europe who had depended on their paychecks.

Hundreds of thousands of New Yorkers worked under awful conditions, and the gap between employer and employee was huge. For a long time, the rich held all the power over these impoverished immigrants and believed they had the right to that power. It took time for the working class to realize that if they joined together—organized and presented a united front to their bosses—they could be more successful in getting what they wanted. Gradually, women began to join men and lobby to improve workplace conditions. And once they managed to organize, which they did remarkably well (considering their lack of education, role models, money, or common language), they fought successfully for improved wages, working conditions, and hours.

3 Early Attempts at Workplace Reform

As early as the 1700s, workers in America realized the benefit of organizing into groups to lobby for changes in the workplace. They joined together to take grievances such as long hours, low pay, and unsafe working conditions to their boss. This group request, or collective bargaining, helped employees have some say in the way they spent their days and earned a living. It was important for them to get and stay organized, so they would be taken seriously by the industry owner. Smart business owners realized that happy, safe workers were more productive and that increased productivity inside the workplace produced benefits outside as well.

The earliest unions were made up of workers from the same type of business or trade. In fact, the first real strike was in 1799 in Philadelphia, led by members of the shoemakers' trade union. Printers, tailors, shipbuilders, hatmakers, railroad workers, cigar makers, carpenters, and other tradesmen soon formed their own trade unions. Gradually, national movements took shape. Some of the first concerns raised by these new unions included rules imposed on apprentices, the regulation of hours and pay, and the desire to form union shops.

Union shops meant that all employees belonged to the union. Union members soon realized the need for dues to establish a fund that could help support the families of striking workers and pay union officers a small salary. Lobbying efforts also began, requesting laws be passed to protect striking workers.

Children often worked as hard as their elders. They usually worked six days a week, 10 hours a day, and earned as little as 50 cents a week. Children were maimed and even killed while working under dangerous conditions in factories and on farms, and there were no laws regulating child labor. By the

To see young boys working at midnight in a glass factory was not unusual. When parents were unable to work or did not make enough money to support the basic needs of their families, their children took low-paying jobs that were grueling even for adults. Eventually, child labor and education laws forced children out of the factories and into schools, but that did not prevent them from working at home late into the night.

early 1800s, many people had begun to speak out against putting young children to work, but still, little was done to change the system. Those being exploited had little or no say in the matter because they were poor. They were afraid that if they spoke up too loudly they would lose their jobs. As bad as their jobs might be, they still needed to work.

This was the case at the Triangle Company, where women and children were paid the least. They had experience doing piecework from home and simply exchanged the location in which they did their work—from the kitchen table to the cramped workspaces of tenement factories. There was a huge economic gap between the factory's owners and its employees. The owners lived in large, well-kept homes; were well fed; wore the latest fashions; were well educated; and had the means to send their children to the best schools. The employees had lives that were exactly the opposite. These differences were obvious to the workers and made them angry. They felt that they worked hard, and all they wanted was a chance to live decent lives in return for that hard work.

For several years before the tragedy at the Triangle Factory, the garment industry had seen the effects of an energized labor movement that started in New York and moved slowly around the country. In 1910, there had been 42 fires in shirtwaist factories alone. Some reformers tried to get laws changed and equipment within the factories updated, but many factory owners and managers figured out ways around the regulations. A massive strike in 1909 improved conditions in some factories, but it was only after the Triangle Factory fire in 1911 that anything concrete was done to improve conditions in all the garment factories.

WOMEN AND UNIONS

In the early days of the unions, men were the only members because women simply did not work in jobs that were unionized. Most men did not believe that women should even work outside of the home, so there was strong resistance to allowing women into unions at all. Gradually, though, women began to take responsibility for their own working conditions and started their own unions, especially in the garment industry. In 1824, in Pawtucket, Rhode Island, workers including about 100 female weavers went on strike to protest an increase in their work hours and a cut in pay. The first all-female strike was held in 1831 by the members of the United Tailoresses Society of New York, which had been formed in 1825. Approximately 1,600 women struck for higher wages. The strike lasted about five weeks but ultimately was unsuccessful. The women went back to work, and the union fell apart shortly thereafter.

The Lowell (Massachusetts) Female Labor Reform Association, which represented women and girls who worked in the garment mills in the town, won their request for a 10-hour workday when they struck in 1834. This was a major victory. It was bad enough that these "mill girls" had to work long hours for low pay, but, often, unscrupulous factory owners and managers played cruel tricks on their workers, such as stopping the clock or turning back its hands, so the girls would not know how long they had actually worked. Sometimes the owners withheld pay, and there was nothing the workers could do about it except take the smaller amount of money.

The Working Women's Union (WWU) was formed in 1864. With a motto of "Union, hand in hand," this group was like a social organization, holding fund-raisers to help members who were in financial trouble and having get-togethers such as picnics. Funds were set up to help provide for workers who were on strike, so they could continue to feed their families while the strike was in effect. Sometimes representatives from the WWU attended meetings of the New York Trades' Assembly, the large men's union in New York. This union included workers from many different trades and unions. Sewing women also formed unions in Baltimore, Detroit, Chicago, and Philadelphia. The Philadelphia branch was successful in getting a 20 percent pay hike for its members.

Going on strike was always a gamble, because there were plenty of desperate people waiting to take jobs that strikers

Mills

The Concord and Merrimack rivers meet in East Chelmsford, Massachusetts. They come together at the Pawtucket Falls, a 34-foot-high torrent of water. This natural attraction lured two mill owners to the town in 1821. Patrick Tracy Jackson and Nathan Appleton recognized the potential in the powerful waterfall and river to run the machinery of a mill they planned to build there.

The men established the Merrimack Manufacturing Company, which produced cotton and calico. Five years later, in 1826, the town was renamed Lowell, after Francis Cabott Lowell, who had revolutionized the textile industry. He invented a power loom that made it possible to transform raw cotton into finished fabric in one factory. Previously, each step of the process was done in different locations by different people. His invention streamlined the entire production.

Lowell also believed in treating employees well. This philosophy influenced Jackson and Appleton, who built what became a model factory with good working conditions and reasonable wages.

It was not long before a series of mills covered a mile along the shore of the Merrimack River. Canals connected the various buildings and also diverted water from the river to the factories, providing power for the machinery.

might lose. Employers often hired strikebreakers, called scabs, to do the jobs of the striking workers. These scabs were not paid any more than those workers on strike, and they still worked long hours, but for some, having a job—any kind of a job—was better than going hungry.

THE CONTRACTOR SYSTEM

Since before the Civil War, the garment industry had utilized a system of contractors. The system was fairly simple, but it was also unfair to those laborers who worked hard to manufacture the garments in the first place. For example, the government might order a certain number of military uniforms from a factory. The factory would, in turn, order these garments from a contractor (today this is known as subcontracting) and agree to pay him a set price per uniform. The contractor then hired individual workers to make these uniforms but paid them a fraction of what he was making on each one. During the Civil War, female workers visited the White House and appealed to President Lincoln to reform this system. After hundreds attended a public meeting sponsored by the newspaper the *New York Sun*, the Working Women's Protective Union was formed in 1865. Women described how they worked for about 12 hours a day yet earned only 15 cents. They had little time for eating and sleeping, much less for taking proper care of their families. Part of this reform movement involved upper- and middle-class women who helped by paying for the lawyers who advocated for the workers. More than 27,000 women appealed to this union for help between 1865 and 1890, and they received nearly $25,000.

Even though industry continued to grow, competition for new jobs remained high because people continued to move to the cities from the countryside as well as from other countries. This competition meant employers could lower wages with little penalty. Workers knew that if they lost their job, there were other people waiting to take it. Reformers published trade

Picketers fight with scabs during a 1935 factory strike *(above)*. Unions protesting for improved work conditions and benefits often faced the challenge of workers who chose not to strike, or new employees who gladly took the jobs.

publications to encourage workers and to keep them informed about new laws and how unions were advocating for them. These papers included the *Labor Standard*, the *Workingman's Advocate*, *Welcome Workingman*, and the *National Labor Tribune*.

By the late 1860s, the National Labor Union (NLU) had been formed. The NLU wanted to establish an eight-hour work-day, stop employers from bringing in prison inmates to work for free, and restrict immigration. It also urged working women, especially the sewing women, to band together and demand equal pay for equal work. This was around the same time that women began to organize to get the right to vote. The success of these suffragists was important to the sewing women. They knew that if women were allowed to vote, it was more likely that changes would be made—that representatives who would change the laws and support the women's movement would be elected. Although this union lasted only about 10 years, the role it played in raising the public's awareness about unsafe working conditions, especially for women, was invaluable.

In New York City, middle-class women formed the Shirt Sewers' Cooperative Union to help improve wages. They worked to get rid of the contractors who found high-paying contracts but paid their workers a tiny amount. Various unions continued to form and grow, all with the common goal of higher wages, shorter hours, and safer working conditions. The Knights of Labor was started in 1869 in Philadelphia by Uriah Stephens, a Baptist minister and tailor. That group had 750,000 members at its height and was successful in getting railroad owners to increase pay. The American Federation of Labor was formed in 1886 and was composed of small unions of skilled workers. Few women were represented by this union for several reasons: Most women still worked at unskilled labor; they were prevented from getting the necessary training by the male-dominated workforce and by social beliefs that a woman's place was in the home. The union meetings were also held late at night, making it difficult or impossible for women with children at home to attend, and union dues were kept just high enough that the women could not afford them.

As the 1800s turned into the 1900s, more than 5 million women worked outside the home. New inventions made it easier to manufacture goods—the electric light, the telephone, the typewriter, and better systems for transporting goods—and helped move America ahead in its continued industrialization, but all these new wonders had a downside. In 1902, a study by the U.S. Industrial Commission said that too many hours spent working actually decreased rather than increased production.

A 1935 ILGWU walkout fills the streets of the New York City garment district with strikers *(above)*. The Triangle Shirtwaist Fire was a catalyst for the labor movement, as previous strikes and calls for workplace safety standards had been ignored by larger factories and government.

These extra hours led to health problems, more accidents due to worker fatigue, poorly manufactured products, and in the end, higher manufacturing costs. In fact, President Ulysses S. Grant had signed a law in 1870, called the National Eight-Hour Law, that reduced the workday for the same amount of pay. It was time for private industry to do the same. A popular song of the time, sung at union meetings was:

> *We want to feel the sunshine;*
> *We want to smell the flowers;*
> *We're sure that God has willed it,*
> *And we mean to have eight hours.*
> *We're summoning our forces*
> *From shipyard, shop and mill,*
> *Eight hours for work;*
> *Eight hours for rest;*
> *Eight hours for what we will!*

Victoria Sherrow, *The Triangle Factory Fire* (Brookfield, Conn.: Millbrook Press, 1995) p. 25.

KEEPING THE WORKPLACE UNION FREE

Obviously, most business owners did not want their employees joining unions, and some went to great lengths to discourage employees from organizing. Some owners even forced employees to sign a contract promising they would not join a union. This document was called an ironclad. If the employee signed this ironclad and then went ahead and joined a union, that worker would be fired. Sometimes employers made a list of employees who had broken their contract or were otherwise considered to be troublemakers, and they circulated it to other business owners. If your name was on one of these lists, you were considered blacklisted, and you might never find work again. Some employers even went so far as to spread rumors about workers of different nationalities, pitting them against one another, to keep them from getting friendly and ultimately organizing into unions.

Some of these intimidation tactics were successful in keeping women from joining unions, although some women did join in secret, including some women at the Triangle Factory. Eventually, women made up more than half the membership in garment workers' unions. One of the more familiar, the International Ladies' Garment Workers' Union (ILGWU), began in 1900 and included women who made shirtwaists, hats, children's clothes, and other items. Another well-known women's union began in Boston in 1903. The Women's Trade Union League (WTUL) attracted many upper-class women, including Eleanor Roosevelt, who joined in 1922. The WTUL became a prime supporter of garment workers and was especially supportive of the women involved in the Triangle fire. The WTUL made it easier for women by holding meetings near their jobs by hiring female doctors who treated members for free and establishing places for female workers to rest between their shifts.

As the twentieth century began, most workers had more rights than ever before, yet conditions were still inhumane in many of the trades. Perhaps no one group of workers suffered more than the New York City garment workers. As the new century started, conditions began to slowly change for them too.

4. Workplace Struggles Before the Fire

The Triangle Company was owned by Max Blanck and Isaac Harris, who had both immigrated to the United States from Russia as young men. They started their business in a small shop in 1900 and called it the Triangle Waist Company. As the business grew, the men leased space in the Joseph J. Asch Building, a new 10-story high-rise on the corner of Greene Street and Washington Place, just east of Washington Square Park. At the time of the tragedy, the Triangle Company was the largest manufacturer of shirtwaists in the country, employing 500 and making $1 million annually in profits.

The site was designated a New York City landmark in 2003 by the Landmarks Preservation Commission. Today, it contains modern offices, with a plaque posted to commemorate those who died in the fire.

This factory made just one product—the shirtwaist. One of the most popular forms of women's clothing for nearly a decade, the shirtwaist was similar to a man's dress shirt, with a collar and long sleeves, but it had a narrow waist and buttons down the back and was considered quite fashionable. The big difference was its fancy style. Many had puffy sleeves, large lace collars, and decorative stitching. The shirtwaist was most often worn with a long, dark skirt and was as common then as T-shirts are today. Part of its appeal was comfort as well as price. They were affordable enough that even lower-class women could buy them. Plus, they were just as acceptable for everyday wear as for church or synagogue.

A TYPICAL FACTORY?

The Triangle Factory was, in many ways, typical of garment factories of the day, which means it was overcrowded and lacked ventilation, light, and other comforts. Cutters used sharp scissors to cut out patterns and cloth. Women sat hunched over sewing machines, painstakingly stitching sleeves and collars onto the bodies of the blouses. Others squinted in the dim light as they sewed on button after button. And still others did finishing work, making sure hems were even, stray threads were snipped, and the final product looked presentable and ready to wear. Very often, the women were paid by the piece. After the constant repetition of sewing the same part of the shirtwaist over and over, these pieceworkers would become very fast at completing their section. When that happened and they were able to complete increasingly more garments in a day, they were not rewarded for their efficiency. Instead, their payment per piece was often lowered, so they ended up making the same amount for more work.

Throughout the day, workers were watched closely by factory managers who walked around to make sure that the seamstresses were working as quickly and accurately as possible. If someone needed a bathroom break, she would have to get permission, and then would be let in and out through a door that was often locked. Sometimes the managers even timed how long the women were gone. As hard as it is to believe, employees sometimes had to bring their own supplies from home or were charged for their supplies—paying out of their meager paychecks for thread, needles, and even

Before machines for cutting patterns were developed, garment factories employed men to cut stacks of cloth into pieces for women to sew together. *Above*, cloth scraps litter the floor of a cutting room in Buffalo, New York. It is not surprising that the Triangle Shirtwaist Factory fire is believed to have started in a flammable pile of scrap cloth.

the electricity to run the sewing machines. In some factories, managers charged employees to hang up their coats and for the chairs on which they sat!

Workplace safety was not as strict as it is today. Many people routinely were injured or even killed in the course of their work. Some estimates quote up to 100 people dying every day on the job! It does not seem like working at a sewing machine would be all that dangerous, but for a number of reasons, it often was. Sometimes it was a factory owner's greed—failing to install safety features such as sprinklers, for example, to save money. Others blamed poor conditions on the police and legal system that did not enforce the laws regulating safety at work. In the case of the Triangle Factory fire of 1911, it was a combination of greed, noncompliance with regulations, and laws that were not enforced, on top of whatever actually happened to start the fire that afternoon.

Today, even the youngest schoolchildren take part in fire drills so they will know what to do in case of a fire. But at the Triangle, as at most other factories, there were no fire drills. And even though fires were common in these garment factories, there were no sprinklers or fire extinguishers. Cloth and paper for patterns were everywhere, as were bits of scrap material and thread. Chairs and tables were all made of wood, and other flammable materials were present. Gas lamps were sometimes used for light, and many people smoked. The sewing machines often had electrical shorts that caused sparks to

Sweatshops

From *Leslie's Illustrated Weekly* 1910:

Pass along any of our great commercial thoroughfares and you will see displayed in the show windows suits of clothes for sale at $5, $6, $8, $9, and $10. You marvel, "How can they do it?" . . . A sweatshop is a place where clothing is made for the big dealers at the prices that enable them to undersell their rivals and offer garments so wonderfully cheap, and it is in addition a graveyard for youth and hope.

fly. Given these conditions, it is really not surprising that fires broke out regularly. During the investigation after the fire, surviving employees talked about the several small fires that had started there previously but had been put out by employees without much damage being done.

At the Triangle and another factory owned by Max Blanck and Isaac Harris, suspicious fires had broken out in 1902, in 1907, and again in 1910. These earlier blazes happened when the factories were closed; no one was hurt, but the insurance company that covered these shops ended up paying out large amounts for material and equipment that were destroyed or damaged. Some speculate that Blanck and Harris did not install fire sprinklers and fire extinguishers on purpose, and instead took out large insurance policies that would cover them in the event of a fire.

THE FACTORY'S LAYOUT

One whole floor, in this case, the eighth floor, was used as the cutting room. This is where cloth was spread across long tables. Patterns were pinned to the cloth, and then cut out. Usually the male employees did this job, because they were stronger and could cut out many layers of cloth at one time. They would cut out the front, back, sleeves, and collars of the shirtwaists and place them in piles to go to the next station.

William L. Beers, the fire marshal who testified in the hearing about the fire later that year, described the fire as starting in this room:

> The result of my investigation and the taking of testimony
> for ten days after the fire was that I was of the opinion that
> the fire occurred on the eighth floor on the Greene Street
> side, under a cutting table, which table was enclosed and
> that contained the waste material as cut from this lawn
> (cloth) that was used to make up the (shirt)waists. They
> were in the habit of cutting about 160 to 180 thicknesses

The formation of the International Ladies' Garment Workers' Union (ILGWU) launched a historic strike called "The Uprising of 20,000," made up of mostly Jewish and Italian immigrant women. With 20,000 striking workers in the street, smaller factories folded to the union's demands within 48 hours, but the Triangle Shirtwaist Factory held out for several months before negotiating an agreement with its workers. *Above*, two strikers stand in solidarity.

of lawn (material) at one time; that formed quite a lot of waste, which was placed under the cutting tables, as it had a commercial value of about seven cents a pound.

He went on to explain that this waste material was tossed into a wooden receptacle under the table formed by boards nailed to the table legs—a perfect fire starter if someone did throw a match.

The ninth floor was crowded with more than 250 sewing machines laid out in 16 narrow rows. Workers' chairs were placed back to back; they were packed tightly into this small space. The lighting was poor here, and there was little ventilation or fresh air. During the summer heat and the freezing winters, these sewing women suffered from the extreme temperatures. Their bodies must have gotten very tired and sore from maintaining the same bent position for 10 or 12 hours every day. Their eyesight suffered, and they often caught colds. And they endured all this for less than $20 a week. The youngest workers worked on this floor. The children cut thread for the women and then threaded their needles. They ran errands and sorted buttons, all for about $1.50 a week. Some of the children trimmed loose threads and were known as cleaners. When they finished with each garment, they put it in a large bin—the same bin they hid in if inspectors came around. Even though there were laws prohibiting children under 14 from working in such conditions, factory owners often broke those laws. Children could sometimes work their way up the ladder to sewing on buttons and by age 16 might actually join the sewing women at a sewing machine, earning by then about $12 a week. But most of the Triangle Factory workers were young women between 13 and 23 years who were from Italy or who were Jews from various European countries.

FACTORY ALREADY NOTORIOUS

The Triangle Shirtwaist Factory and its owners were already known in the industry—and not in a good way. In 1909, shirtwaist workers around New York City went on strike in what became known as the Uprising of 20,000 (from November 1909 to February 1910). Because it was the industry's busy season, many of the other shirtwaist factory owners gave in to employees' demands for more pay, fewer hours, and recognition of the union—especially the small factories that could not survive for long if their workers were not working. But owners of some of the larger factories, including the Triangle Factory, formed an alliance of their own. They called it the Employers' Mutual

Protection Association. Led by the Triangle owners, members placed ads in newspapers for scabs, offered extra pay to workers to stay on the job, and hired men to attack the employees who did walk the picket lines. There was little sympathy from police or judges, who arrested many of the strikers and sent them to jail. The Triangle owners never gave in, even though the original walkout that led to the strike began there.

THE UPRISING OF 20,000

Thousands of garment workers filled the meeting hall when Local 25 of the International Ladies' Garment Workers' Union (ILGWU) held a meeting on November 22, 1909, to discuss a general strike. For months, factory owners had increased their hours of operation while holding the pay rate the same. Several hundred workers were already on strike, and now the union was considering bringing all its members into it. A young woman, 19-year old Clara Lemlich, was in attendance that night, and she listened with growing dismay as speaker after speaker rose to urge caution. A month or so before, she had been badly beaten, to the point of having to be hospitalized, by attackers who wanted her to reduce her union involvement. After Samuel Gompers, the president of the American Federation of Labor (AFL) spoke, the crowd was excited and expected a vote to be taken. Instead, yet another speaker stood up.

A frustrated Clara ran to the podium. She called out loudly in Yiddish, "I want to say a few words!" She went on: "I have no further patience for talk as I am one of those who feels and suffers from the things pictured. I move that we go on a general strike...now!" The audience cheered, and then the issue was put to a vote. The strike began the next morning with more than 15,000 participants; they demanded a 20 percent raise, a 52-hour workweek, and overtime pay. By the day after that, 20,000 workers from 500 factories were involved in the strike.

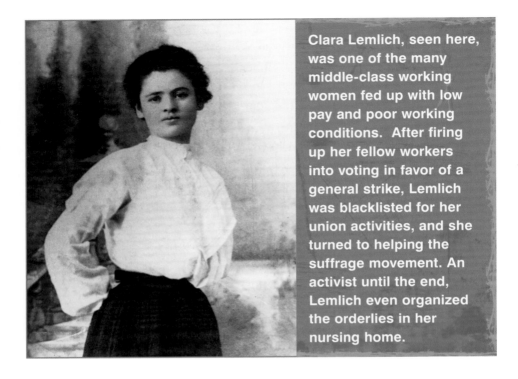

Clara Lemlich, seen here, was one of the many middle-class working women fed up with low pay and poor working conditions. After firing up her fellow workers into voting in favor of a general strike, Lemlich was blacklisted for her union activities, and she turned to helping the suffrage movement. An activist until the end, Lemlich even organized the orderlies in her nursing home.

At some point during this strike, some wealthy women who were socially progressive joined the cause of the striking women by organizing rallies and giving them money. Anne Morgan, the daughter of J.P. Morgan, famous for his steel mills, was one of the most well known. Another was Alva Belmont, whose first husband was William Vanderbilt, a businessman who had inherited more than $100 million from his father. Their involvement brought more attention to the strikers' demands, as newspapers became aware of what was happening. Also, when these well-to-do women appeared at the picket lines, the police were less likely to treat the picketers roughly. These women who stepped up to help the poor strikers believed that this was part of the larger cause to improve the rights of all women in the country—rich or poor. They also believed that all women would have better lives if they had the right to vote. They arranged rallies and fund-raising events and provided priceless emotional support.

The Triangle fire tragedy was deeply felt, in part, because of these events only a year before. Had the strike of winter 1909–1910 been completely successful, the subsequent reforms may have prevented the senseless loss of life on March 25, 1911. What happened that day led activists to become even more forceful in pushing for changes in legislation that would prevent such a calamity from ever happening again.

David Von Drehle writes in his book *Triangle: The Fire That Changed America*, "The Triangle was a good example of what we would call a sweatshop today—a big crowded factory with workers at long tables, but the workers would not have thought of themselves as being in a sweatshop. To them sweatshops were tiny tenement factories of ten or 12 people, with no light, electricity, or plumbing." What irony that this "modern" factory with electricity and elevators and plenty of work was home to one of the worst workplace disasters to ever take place in this country.

5 Day of Tragedy

Saturday morning—March 25, 1911—dawned clear, bright, and mild. Springtime had come to New York City, leaving behind winter's grayness. Even though it was a Saturday, thousands of city dwellers woke early to prepare for work. Pushcart peddlers shouted at passersby to get their fruit and vegetables. Bakers were in their shops sweating over ovens to prepare bread for customers. And many people were dressing to go to work in one of the hundreds of garment factories located around the city.

The several hundred employees who worked Saturdays at the Triangle Shirtwaist Factory headed there and got down to work just like normal. Shortly after 4:30 P.M. on March 25, the workers were finishing up their nine-hour day and preparing to leave when someone yelled "Fire!" The exact cause of the fire remains unknown, although survivors testified later that it seemed like the fire just came up at them from under the tables. Possibly an electrical short in one of the sewing machines was to blame, or perhaps someone tossed a match or smoldering cigarette on the floor too close to a pile of fabric. Oil for the machines, piles and baskets of fabric, finished shirtwaists, bits of lace, and paper patterns provided ready fuel for the blaze, which started on the eighth floor and spread rapidly. The last pickup of scrap material—of more than a ton—had been on January 15. It is estimated that there was at least another ton of material in the factory that day.

Most of the employees from the eighth floor—the material cutters—had already left, leaving material and patterns spread out on the tables, ready for Monday morning. About 100 women from the eighth floor were lining up to leave, waiting their turn to have their purses checked for stolen supplies—a standard practice—by the managers as they moved through the doorway. As quickly as possible, these women fled through the door, but the hallway was very narrow and lined with large bins filled with rags and material. A switchboard operator on the eighth floor reportedly tried to call up to the ninth floor, but no one answered the phone. She did reach the tenth floor and warned workers about the fire. The factory's owners were at work in the administrative offices on this floor, and they were able to escape by climbing the stairs to the roof. Another administrative worker called the fire department. The first alarm was sounded at 4:30 P.M. Three more alarms were sounded by Fire Battalion Chief Edward J. Worth at 4:48, 4:55, and 5:10 P.M.

The fire began on the Greene Street side of the building, where the one set of stairs that led to the roof was located. Fortunately for the workers on the eighth and tenth floors, the doors to the stairs were unlocked, and many escaped through them and went up to the roof. Those that made it to the roof were helped to the adjacent New York University building by students there. Then, they were able to make it to the street safely. Unfortunately, those women still at work on the ninth floor who tried to escape through the fire door found it locked. The fire was concentrated on the opposite side of the room, where the only open door was located. Most of those who died had been working on this floor.

During the investigation after the fire, many people mentioned the fact that doors were locked. In their testimony,

Factory owners often pushed sewing machines close together to pack in as many workers as possible. This limited and even cut off escape routes. *Above*, the sewing floor of a Troy, New York, factory holds hundreds of employees.

Max Blanck and Isaac Harris said that locking one of the two doors was standard practice so that the factory managers could check the women's purses. It is not known whether they had reason to believe their employees were thieves, but they made their statements matter-of-factly, as if locking workers in was not a big deal.

Initially, buckets were filled from an open barrel of water to try to put out the fire. A hose was dragged in from the hallway, but there was barely any water pressure, and the women quickly realized they needed to think about escaping rather than extinguishing the fire. The cramped conditions and thick smoke must have made it difficult to figure out the best way to get off the ninth floor. There were no fire sprinklers in the Triangle Factory. There also were no modern fire extinguishers, and there was too much fuel lying about feeding this fire for a few buckets of water to do much good. There was only one fire escape, and it was rusty and rickety and ended fairly high off the ground. Between the fire's heat and the weight of many women trying to get down at once, the old structure gave way, falling to the ground and taking the women with it. Only about 20 women survived by using the fire escape.

"The Uprising of the Twenty Thousand"

A song dedicated to the Waistmakers of 1909:

In the black of the winter of nineteen nine,
When we froze and bled on the picket line,
We showed the world that women could fight,
And we rose and won with women's might.

Hail the Waistmakers of nineteen nine,
Making their stand on the picket line,
Breaking the power of those who reign
Pointing the way, smashing the chain

And we gave new courage to the men
Who carried on in nineteen ten,
And shoulder-to-shoulder we'll win through
Led by the I.L.G.W.U.

There were four working elevators in the Asch Building, two for passengers and two for freight. The elevator serving the Greene Street side of the building was big enough for only about 15 passengers at one time. Of course, many more than 15 women tried to cram into the small space; some even climbed on top of the box as it descended, overloading the elevator and breaking the cable. It was unable to go back up to rescue more women. All this chaos and confusion happened quickly, with women running about, screaming and beating at flames. Survivors remember it as a flash, and in fact, most of the worst of the damage was done in less than 20 minutes.

OUTSIDE

The scene in the street was horrifying for onlookers. This was a tight-knit community where many of those watching had relatives and friends working inside the factory. As fire engines raced to the scene, people arrived and frantically began searching for loved ones. Police tried to keep people away from the sidewalk, where debris, ash, and bodies were falling. People looked up in shock to the windows where dozens of women were clinging as smoke billowed around them and flames licked at their long skirts and hair. Many of these women either jumped or fell out of open windows, in spite of the firemen's attempts to rescue them. Some of the onlookers held tightly onto the corners of blankets, calling out for women to jump and they would catch them. Mostly, this did not work, as the weight of the falling young women pulled the blankets from their hands, and the women hit the pavement. In the twilight, the orange flames illuminated the stranded workers, and many eyewitnesses reported later that some of the girls were crying, others held hands, and some seemed to be praying just before they jumped. A total of 58 workers jumped or fell to their deaths. There were even reports of one male employee helping several women out of the windows, so they could jump

Fire ladders failed to reach the ninth floor of the Triangle Shirtwaist Factory and safety nets broke under the weight of the girls jumping from windows.

rather than be burned to death. Reportedly, the final woman he helped escape was his fiancée, and they kissed tenderly before they both plunged to the sidewalk below.

William G. Shepherd was a wire service reporter who happened to be in the area of the Asch Building when the fire broke out. He wrote an account of what he saw, which was published two days later in the *Milwaukee Journal*.

> As I reached the scene of the fire, a cloud of smoke hung over the building. I looked up to the seventh floor. There was a living picture in each window—four screaming heads of girls waving their arms.
>
> "Call the firemen," they screamed—scores of them. "Get a ladder," cried others. They were all as alive and whole and sound as were we who stood on the sidewalk. I couldn't help thinking of that. We cried to them not to jump. We heard the siren of a fire engine in the distance. The other sirens sounded from several directions.
>
> "Here they come," we yelled. "Don't jump; stay there."
>
> One girl climbed onto the window sash. Those behind her tried to hold her back. Then she dropped into space. *(Source: www.ilr.cornell.edu)*

Within 10 minutes of the phone call to the fire department, Engine Company Nos. 18 and 72 and Hook and Ladder Company No. 20 arrived. They had some new equipment, including high-pressure hoses and two engines that were motorized; most fire engines at that time were still pulled by teams of horses. More than 30 engines responded to the fire. A special 20-foot net supported by a steel frame was spread out to catch the women, but just as with the blankets and other nets used by firefighters that day, the material was not strong enough to catch several women jumping at once. The tallest ladder on one truck was pulled out and extended up the side of the building, but it reached only to about the sixth floor. Some firefighters climbed the ladder anyway, trying to scramble up the outside of the building to rescue the women but were unable to do so. Some others went up the inside stairwell, dragging hoses with them. These men were able to put out the fire fairly quickly once they broke through the locked doors that had prevented the women's escape.

William Shepherd's report continued:

> The firemen began to raise a ladder. Others took out a life net and, while they were rushing to the sidewalk with it, two more girls shot down. The firemen held it under them; the bodies broke it . . . The firemen raised the longest ladder. It reached only to the sixth floor. I saw the last girl jump at it and miss it. And then the faces disappeared from the window. But now the crowd was enormous, though all this had occurred in less than seven minutes, the start of the fire and the thuds and deaths.

Police patrols were called in to maintain order among the crowd and help anxious friends and relatives search for survivors. According to the *New York Times*, the firemen had trouble getting their equipment in place both because of the crowd watching and the dead employees stacked on the sidewalk.

In total, 146 people lost their lives at the factory that day, most from the fire and smoke inhalation and the rest from falling or jumping to their deaths. The enormity of the tragedy angered the community, and that outrage quickly extended throughout the city and then the country.

6 The Fire's Aftermath

As night began to fall, more and more people continued to arrive on the scene, desperately searching for familiar faces. Cries of grief went out mostly in Italian and Yiddish as victims were found. But it was almost impossible to identify many of the bodies because of the extensive burns and damage done during the falls. Often, relatives were able to identify someone only by a piece of jewelry. Initially, the police covered the bodies on the sidewalks with blankets and tarps. But then horse-drawn wagons were used to carry the bodies to a temporary morgue located on Misery Lane on the Twenty-Sixth Street Pier on the East River.

The sight greeting firemen inside the Asch Building was as sad and gruesome as that outside. Many employees caught in the flames of the fast-moving fire or overcome by smoke had barely had time to move, and some were even found still at their workstations. Most were unrecognizable. Despite the intensity and ferocity of the fire, 24 wedding and engagement rings were later found among the ashes.

The police tied numbered tags to the bodies, and the reporter William Shepherd wrote later that this was when he remembered that these were the shirtwaist makers, and perhaps he also recognized the terrible irony. According to Sherrow, he wrote, "I recalled their great strike of last year in which these same girls had demanded more sanitary conditions and more safety precautions in the shops. These dead bodies were the answer."

At one point, 2,000 people waited to enter the morgue, even though only 20 or so were allowed in at a time. It took all night for the bodies to arrive at the morgue and days before they were all claimed. Seven bodies never were identified. Throughout the city, people's emotions were raw. Unbelievable sadness mixed with anger. Newspapers ran banner headlines and long stories including passages with quotes from eyewitnesses. Some people wondered how this tragedy could have happened, while others pointed a finger at corrupt politicians, police, and courts; inspectors who did not uphold regulations; and factory owners who seemed to have total disregard for those they employed.

The *New York Times* reported the following day:

> The victims who are now lying at the Morgue waiting for some one to identify them by a tooth or the remains of a burned shoe were mostly girls from 16 to 23 years of age. They were employed at making shirtwaist by the Triangle Waist Company, the principal owners of which are Isaac Harris and Max Blanck. Most of them could barely speak English. Many of them came from Brooklyn. Almost all were the main support of their hard-working families.

Within a week, union officials were calling for new legislation on workplace safety, even as they honored the dead. The Waistmakers' Union held a funeral for those victims who remained unidentified, and it planned a march to honor all those who had died. On a cold, rainy day, April 5, 1911,

Families of the fire victims wander through a temporary morgue to identify their loved ones. Because the victims were so badly burned, identification was done through clothing, jewelry, or letters the victims were carrying at the time of the fire. Seven bodies remained unidentified, and thousands of mourners attended their funeral procession.

thousands of mourners representing 60 trade unions met at Washington Square. Marching behind an empty hearse that symbolized all the victims, they made their way though the stone arch at Washington Square and up Fifth Avenue, where purple and black cloths were hung in mourning from doorways and windows. Hundreds of thousands lined the streets in a solemn tribute. Everyone who participated as a marcher or onlooker knew this gathering was also a protest against unsafe working conditions. Banners were held up that spoke of sorrow but also called for change. One read, "We Demand Fire Protection!"

Money soon started pouring into different funds established right after the fire. The International Ladies' Garment Workers' Union Local 25 quickly started a fund-raising effort to help the families of the victims. This union raised $120,000. The Red Cross collected another $100,000. The mayor of New York City formed a committee to coordinate the various fund-raising efforts and to interview survivors and victims' families to find out what they needed most. Some of those who were killed were the sole providers for their families, and their deaths devastated those left behind, not only emotionally, but also financially.

TURNING TRAGEDY AROUND

After the funerals, life in the Lower East Side slowly returned to normal except for the outrage against the owners of the Triangle Factory and others like it. Grief soon turned to determination to prevent something similar from ever happening again. A meeting was held by the Women's Trade Union League during which many speakers addressed the crowd, begging for legal reforms and better factory inspections. These working-class people knew now that they had to work closely together to make new laws a reality and could not rely on the factory owners and managers to look out for them.

Family members of the victims attended another meeting, which turned the event into something sadly personal. Everyone there was united by their need to make some sense of what was a senseless disaster. One of the speakers at this gathering was Dr. Anna Shaw, a leader in the growing women's rights movement. Sherrow quotes Shaw as saying: "Every man and woman is responsible. You men . . . as voters it was your business . . . if you are incompetent, then in the name of heaven, stand aside and let us try. . . . women can not regulate her own conditions, her own hours of labor. She has been driven into the market with no voice in laws and powerless to defend

First Person

One of the young survivors of the fire testified to the horror she encountered in the factory that afternoon.

Rosie Safran said she ran for the door on the Washington Place side of the building as soon as she heard someone yell, "Fire!" That door was locked, and girls trying to escape quickly created a logjam in front of it. The fire was concentrated at that time on the opposite side of the room, and so they could not get to the one door that was left unlocked. She stated that the doors were normally locked all the time.

The girls realized that the fire was spreading and growing very quickly and that they were in real danger of being burned to death. Girls were screaming for help and beating at the door, the top of which was glass. Rosie testified that someone broke the glass and she managed to climb through and run down the stairs to the sixth floor, at which point she was led outside to safety.

herself. The most cowardly thing that men ever did was when they tied women's hands and left her to be food for the flames." A former sweatshop employee turned lawyer, Morris Hillquit, closed the meeting by encouraging the audience to work hard to change the laws. He said, "The greatest monument we can raise to the memory of our 146 dead is a system of legislation which will make such deaths hereafter impossible."

CALLING FOR JUSTICE

The week after the march, Max Blanck and Isaac Harris were arrested and charged with manslaughter. They hired

Max D. Steuer to represent them, and the men went to trial in early December 1911. More than 150 witnesses testified. One survivor told how she and a friend had tried to open the door to the ninth-floor stairwell but could not. The witness, Kate Alderman, described how she was able to escape by wrapping herself in a coat and some material to protect herself as she ran through the fire. Her friend did not make it out.

William L. Beers, the city's fire marshal was asked how the fire could have started, and he answered:

Protesters march through the streets of New York after the tragedy *(above)*. They called for new labor reforms, support for the victims' families, and punishment for the owners of the Triangle Waist Company.

Well, we formed the opinion that it started from the careless use of a match from one of the cutters. They were about to leave to go home, and in those factories they are very anxious to get a smoke just as quick as they get through work ... and carelessly threw it under there; then the attention of the occupants was called to it, and they tried to extinguish it before they rang in a fire alarm.

He went on to testify that there was only one fire escape at the rear of the building, which was not nearly enough for the number of employees there. He said it was too small and not strong enough, and in addition, the iron shutters covering the fire escape on the building's exterior would have kept the people from being able to pass easily from the platform to the stairs. He also testified that the factory was overcrowded with machines, saying that all the available space was used.

When Beers was asked what recommendations he would make to the city to help prevent such tragedies, he replied:

I think that all manufacturing establishments should have an interior automatic signaling device to call attention to fires when they occur, and they should also have an automatic extinguishing device in the form of sprinklers and of standpipes. Local fire drills should be compulsory and all the exits in factories should be marked, as in theatres, and the factory employees should be drilled the same as the crew of a ship is drilled. The fire station should be known, and the specific duties of each employee should be known in case of fire. That is, some of the men should be directed to get female employees out of the building, and the others should be directed to get the male employees together for the purpose of fighting the fire and holding it in check until such time as assistance came.

I think that here in the city, all these loft buildings that are used for manufacturing purposes, the equipment should be standardized and should be as nearly fireproof as possible, and no tenant should be permitted to occupy a building of that kind without first filing a plan showing the way in which the manufacturing apparatus is to be installed, and that should be as near fireproof as possible; and he should not be permitted to fill up his building with a lot of combustible material without proper supervision. The number of persons employed in a given area should be specified and approved and the plan of the building, with the exits all marked, should be posted on the walls of the building, so that it would be there and the employees could become familiar with it, and know just where they are to go in case of fire.

Smoking should be absolutely prohibited in such industries as shirtwaist making and light lawn dresses, or where any of those light inflammables are used, chiffons and veilings, straw goods, hat factories, or in any factory using a large quantity of material that is flammable. I think, also, it would be wise to have lectures in the public schools, under the auspices of the Board of Education, instructing these employees what to do in case of fire, especially in schools located in these districts where the factory employees reside. (Source: www.ilr.cornell.edu)

Many of his suggestions were the same or similar to pleas made by the unions during the strike of 1909—requests that had been ignored.

HIGHLIGHTS OF THE CASE

✳ The prosecution and defense argued about whether or not the door on the ninth floor was locked, preventing the workers from escaping.

Inspectors point to the door that would have been a viable escape for the girls trapped in the factory, had the door not been locked. It was common practice for factory owners to lock employees inside until the end of the day, not letting the girls out until they had been searched.

Witnesses for both sides testified, with those for the owners saying the door was unlocked. Some survivors claimed that the door was always kept locked at closing time so managers could search the bags of every employee to ensure no one was stealing goods from the factory. The prosecution also argued that there were quite a few bodies found just inside the door because workers expected to find a way out there, but could not, and they were overcome there by smoke and flame. The lawyers for the defense claimed these victims could not get out because of the fire in the stairwell, not because the door was locked.

* The fire escape was not built to building code specifications. Instead, it ended at a second-floor skylight and was not sturdy enough to support the weight of the escaping workers.

* If the Asch Building had been another 15 feet higher, New York's building codes would have required it to have metal window frames and stone or concrete floors, which would not have burned as quickly as the wood trim and floors that had been used in its construction.

* At the time of the fire, there were no laws requiring sprinklers in New York City buildings, nor were there any laws requiring regular fire drills. There were no sprinklers in the Triangle Factory, and its employees had never had a fire drill.

* According to New York City regulations, the Asch Building should have had three sets of stairs in the building, not two. But an exception was granted to the architect.

* On the ninth floor, 75-foot-long tables crowded the workspace, and aisles were blocked by chairs and baskets. And the stairway, at two feet, nine inches, was too narrow for the doors to open out as the law required.

The judge reminded the jury that even if the door on the ninth floor was locked, there needed to be proof that the owners knew it was locked in order to find them guilty. The all-male jury acquitted Blanck and Harris because it could not do that. The defendants also faced 23 individual suits filed by victims' families. They ended up settling those for about $75 per victim. In March 1912, a second charge of manslaughter was brought against the defendants involving other Triangle victims. These charges were dropped however, based on "double jeopardy," which prohibits someone from being charged more than once for the same crime.

The owners never admitted they had been neglectful in the management of their company or unfair in the treatment of the more than 500 workers. In fact, just days after the devastating fire, Max Blanck and Isaac Harris reopened the factory in another site in the city. They tried to advertise in the local papers for more workers, but public opinion against the two men was so strong the newspapers refused to run the ads. The owners, however, collected $60,000 from the fire insurance policy they had on the factory. Despite this huge settlement, the two men began to lose money and went out of business about 10 years after the fire.

After the disaster, unions continued to grow in number and in strength. The impact of the loss in New York City was felt all over the country. Women fearlessly walked picket lines to improve working conditions and fought tirelessly to gain voting rights. Laws were passed regulating work hours and wages and curtailing the use of young children for menial labor or dangerous factory work. Many reforms were instituted to provide workers with better and safer work conditions. The changes did not happen overnight, but gradually, they came, even to the worst tenement factories.

7 The Fire's Legacy

Factory owners across the city came under close scrutiny after the tragedy on March 25, 1911. Fire inspectors became more diligent in making their rounds and fining those factories that did not comply with fire codes. Building inspectors did likewise. More immigrant workers realized the power of organization and joined unions, which gained not only in numbers but also in strength. Although the depth of the negligence was inexcusable, some good eventually came from the loss of so many lives at the Triangle Factory.

During the year following the fire, the Women's Trade Union League (WTUL) sent out surveys to factory employees around the city. The questionnaire asked for ratings on safety issues such as fire escapes and sprinklers and fire hazards in the workplace. The union kept the survey anonymous so that employees could not be identified and punished for answering honestly. The workers were also asked about ventilation, sanitation, and how many hours they worked. Anything that would have a negative impact on employees' health and safety was covered in the survey.

CONDITIONS BEGIN TO IMPROVE

The laws governing workplace health and safety conditions were inadequate, and the city did a poor job in enforcing those regulations that did exist. The building and fire departments did not coordinate regulation and inspection, and four different departments within city government undertook investigations after the fire: the coroner's office, the district attorney, Fire Commissioner Rhinelander Waldo, and Building Department Superintendent Albert Ludwig. Private organizations also ran investigations, including the New York City Chamber of Commerce and the Architectural League.

The Committee on Safety also formed within days after the fire. Composed of teachers and religious and civic leaders, the committee included such notables as Frances Perkins, future secretary of labor under Franklin D. Roosevelt; Rabbi Stephen Wise; WTUL president Mary Dreier; and Henry Stimson, the future secretary of war during World War II. This committee joined the Women's Trade Union League and the International Ladies' Garment Workers' Union in pushing for investigations into the fire and workplace safety in general, and for legal reforms to ensure such a tragedy would never again happen. The committee traveled to the state capital in Albany and urged their legislators to take action. A fire in the statehouse just a few days after the Triangle fire made these lawmakers more receptive to suggestions involving fire prevention and other safety matters.

Strong lobbying efforts led to the formation of a special Factory Investigating Commission on June 30, 1911, by the New York state legislature. Senator Robert F. Wagner and future New York governor Alfred Smith headed the commission. They began what would turn into the largest, most thorough investigation and evaluation of workplace safety and workers' health ever undertaken. According to the Department of Labor, the commission was to investigate the conditions under which manufacturing was done. The commission was given broad powers, including the ability to call witnesses "to testify under oath about workplace fire hazards, unsanitary conditions, occupational diseases, effectiveness of factory inspection, tenement manufacturing and many other matters." Some powerful people worked diligently on behalf of this commission. In addition to Wagner and Smith as chairman and vice-chairman, Samuel Gompers, president of the American Federation of Labor, helped get various unions to support the commission's work. Head attorney Abram Elkus was scientific and exacting in his questioning of witnesses and gathering of facts. And other notables in the field of health and safety testified and contributed to investigations.

Elkus used the commission's first public hearing on October 11, 1911, to make sure that everyone was aware of the group's goal. He conceded that the Triangle Factory fire had brought to light the need for better safety rules, regulations, and enforcement but that it also enlightened people to another workplace menace—unsanitary conditions that led to disease. According to www.dol.gov, he said, "Industrial diseases have practically been permitted to go unchecked, resulting in the untimely death of thousands." He also said that disease diminished the productivity of the economy and was one of the main causes of poverty among workers and their families.

LAWS PASSED

The investigations continued through 1912. Fifty-nine public hearings were held, with 472 witnesses making appearances. More than 7,000 pages were filled with testimony from employers and employees; union officials; experts in the fields of fire safety, construction, heating, lighting, ventilation; and others. They investigated not only clothing factories but

International Ladies' Garment Workers' Union

The ILGWU was founded in 1900 to represent workers in the garment trade. This union was made up primarily of Jewish immigrants, who were the bulk of workers within this trade, especially in New York City. These immigrants worked long hours in unsafe, unsanitary, and uncomfortable conditions in sweatshops throughout the city. The ranks of the union swelled with even more Jewish immigrants between 1905 and 1910.

The Uprising of 20,000—the first large strike of female garment workers that took place in New York during the winter of 1909–1910—gained a shorter workday and workweek and higher wages for many of the sweatshop workers in the city. The Triangle Factory was one of a handful of businesses whose owners did not give in to the union's demands. Ironically, this strike began at the Triangle.

The union was struggling at this time and left much of the strike management up to the Women's Trade Union League (WTUL), made up of upper- and middle-class volunteers, and the striking workers themselves.

also meatpacking plants, bakeries, printshops, and chemical manufacturers. As a result, the commission recommended that health was indeed the prime concern of all workers and that government should do everything in its power to protect that asset.

The commission drafted 26 bills around health and other worker protection plans, and it submitted 17 of them. Thirteen actually became New York state law, creating strict codes

During the 1970s, membership in the ILGWU shrank, as many textile production companies moved their operations overseas. In 1995, the ILGWU merged with the Amalgamated Clothing and Textile Workers' Union, forming the Union of Needletrades, Industrial and Textile Employees.

The union is a member of the American Federation of Labor and Congress of Industrial Organizations (AFL-CIO), a group that incorporates about 10 million workers within 50 different, independent national and international unions. The AFL was formed in 1886 by Samuel Gompers as a group of craft unions. The CIO was started in 1935 by some of the AFL unions that wanted to organize workers, both skilled and unskilled, within specific industries. It was first known as the Committee for Industrial Organization but changed to its current name at its first convention in 1938. The two merged in 1955.

The AFL-CIO covers diverse types of industries and workers, including actors, airplane pilots, engineers, and machinists. Its combined force has improved working conditions, pay, and benefits for millions since its inception more than 100 years ago.

around fire safety, sanitation, ventilation, safer elevators, and guards on various types of machinery. In October 1911, the first new legislation was passed dealing specifically with one of the causes of the Triangle fire. The Sullivan-Hoey Fire Prevention Law established a powerful Fire Commission in New York City. This commission took on the responsibilities that had previously been handled by six separate agencies. Factory owners now had to install automatic sprinklers and keep them in good working order. The law also established a Division of Fire Prevention whose duties were mainly centered on inspection of buildings for unsafe practices and education of business owners and employers on ways to stop a fire from ever starting.

Groups representing business and industry tried to weaken these laws but actually may have served to strengthen them. During the four years between the inception of the

President Roosevelt *(above)* signs the Wagner Act, also known as National Labor Relations Act. Before this bill, workers had no protection from their employers, and there were constant clashes during strikes between unions and the police and security that supported the factories. By passing the Wagner Act, the U.S. government allowed the formation of unions without reprisals from employers.

commission and the adoption of the 20th and final law in 1915, the work of the commission raised public awareness to the extent of the serious problems in many aspects of U.S. industry. Some have called these four years a golden era in New York because of the light shed on a difficult topic. According to www.dol.gov, Frances Perkins called the Factory Investigating Commission "a turning point in American attitudes toward social responsibility," saying the flames of the Triangle fire were magnified into "a torch that lighted up the industrial scene."

As the bills were introduced and laws passed, the Women's Trade Union League (WTUL) kept its members and other workers informed by holding meetings and publishing information in labor newspapers. Workers were encouraged to report any violations to the WTUL, which started the School for Active Workers in the Labor Movement in 1914; this school trained workers to be leaders in the reform movement within their industries.

THE PROGRESSIVE ERA

In the United States, the period from the 1890s through the 1920s is known as the Progressive Era for all the social and workplace reforms that took place. A prime resource for unions and employees during this time was the American Federation of Labor (AFL). Formed in 1886 by Samuel Gompers, who remained its president until 1924, it was the largest organization of unions in the country. The AFL was 30 years old in 1911, by which time it represented more than half of all workers who belonged to unions. Its prime concern was with working conditions and pay, and it tried hard to address individual worker and union demands and concerns without getting caught up in politics. Blacks, Asians, and women were generally excluded from membership in the AFL, as in most unions. Individuals within the union struggled to change this segregation, and after the fire, more unions became open to admitting minorities.

Those behind the Progressive Movement, including reformers Alfred Smith and Robert Wagner, later U.S. senator from New York, as well as a young Senator Franklin D. Roosevelt, felt reform was needed in several areas. They wanted to change the way politicians were elected; they pushed for economic reforms; and they wanted more equality and social justice. They were focused especially on setting limits on how much money people could give to political candidates, the process for passing laws, and rules on congressional debates. Many were concerned about the fate of immigrants—especially poor immigrants clustered in cities.

PUBLIC AWARENESS IS RAISED

Journalists and novelists also had been working to raise public awareness about social inequality and corruption in business and government. In addition, they wrote about such topics as child labor, safety, women, and tenement factories. Journalists who exposed the underside of American life and business were known as *muckrakers*, a term coined by President Theodore Roosevelt after a character in the book *Pilgrim's Progress*. These magazines that published stories about social injustices also printed editorial cartoons about politicians and other well-known figures, and serials, stories that continued from month to month. The public loved them. Authors such as Upton Sinclair also helped teach the public about what was going on in the world around them. In 1906, Sinclair wrote one of the most famous books of the era, *The Jungle*. The book was about dangerous conditions in the meatpacking industry. Others wrote about the link between industry and big business and government, claiming corruption and unfair business practices. The more people read about social injustices and inequalities, the more outspoken they became.

On-the-job safety was just wishful thinking around 1900. Hundreds were killed in the railroad and mining industries, and more than 50,000 accidents happened in New York City factories between 1900 and 1909. Safety experts concluded

After the fire of a supposedly "fireproof" building claimed 146 lives, officials pushed for stronger education in fire safety and prevention. Here, a poster made by the Tenement House Department reminds citizens to keep their fire escapes free of obstacles.

the number of New York City accidents could have been cut by two-thirds with the implementation of simple precautions such as lighted and wider halls and stairwells, working fire escapes, enclosed passenger elevators, and safety guards on machinery. Often, when someone was injured or killed on the job, the report blamed it on employee error. Negligence or refusal to obey safety codes on the part of the owners was rarely mentioned. There was no such thing as workers' compensation. Today, if someone is injured on the job and cannot work, he or she can collect workers' compensation benefits. This money is a percentage of an employee's pay, meant to help support his or her family while the employee is out of work. Early attempts at workers' compensation laws in Maryland, Montana, and New York were declared unconstitutional because they deprived employers of their property—meaning their employee. The courts often decided for the employer, saying that a worker in a dangerous job knew the risks when he or she took the job.

There is no doubt that the Triangle fire is one of the worst workplace tragedies in U.S. history and that it changed forever the American workplace. One of the most lasting effects has been the enactment of a network of laws governing workplace conditions. Regulations that are commonplace today include some items that seem so simple now but that in 1911 were not. Clear paths to all exits, several fire exits, and unlocked doors are now routine. Offices and factories must have fire extinguishers and other firefighting equipment, and employees have to be trained in their use. All rooms must have fire sprinklers. Businesses have to hold regular fire drills and post emergency plans for evacuating the building. The Occupational Safety and Health Act, which covers these rules and many others, was signed by President Richard Nixon on December 29, 1970. The Occupational Safety and Health Administration today regulates all workplace health and safety issues by issuing certain standards covering injuries on the job, illnesses, and deaths.

After the fire, politicians knew they could no longer practice a laissez-faire, or hands-off, approach to business. Before 1911, government avoided placing too many rules and regulations on businesspeople, believing the marketplace would regulate itself and counting on honest business owners to govern themselves. After March 25, 1911, they could no longer avoid putting laws in place to protect workers. After New York began legislating the workplace, other states followed. New York lawmakers were influenced in their efforts by the International Ladies' Garment Workers' Union that authorized a march of 100,000 seeking action. Samuel Gompers, president of the AFL, served on the Factory Commission of 1911, giving him a front-row seat to the process by which the laws were selected and put into place and allowing him to advocate for union members.

Accidents caused by neglect and disregard for the laws, unfortunately, still happen. On March 25, 1990—the 79th anniversary of the Triangle fire—a fire at a Bronx, New York, social club killed 87 people. These were not workers, but customers. Although the fire was arson, set by a drunken and disgruntled man, the owners had disregarded earlier fire department citations and had not installed a sprinkler system or fire alarm. In addition, the windows were barred, and there was only one escape door. The following year, 25 workers were killed in a North Carolina poultry factory fire caused by malfunctioning machinery. Somehow inspectors had missed this factory, and more than 75 workers were killed and injured because of locked exit doors.

SWEATSHOPS

By the end of World War II, sweatshops had all but disappeared thanks to increased and stronger regulations and more powerful and effective unions. Unfortunately, they have become more common again in the past 25 years as the world's economy has globalized. Businesses that at one time were confined to one region can now open factories anywhere in the world. In many cases, this means opening offices or factories—sweatshops—where they can find low-cost laborers whose rights are ignored by dictators or other governments who do not put their peoples' interests first.

If a workplace breaks two or more basic laws established through the U.S. Department of Labor, including minimum wage, fire safety, and child labor, it is considered to be a sweatshop. Often these places refuse to hire people who belong to unions and refuse to allow employees to organize. According to Department of Labor statistics, as many as 50 percent of today's garment factories in the United States can be considered sweatshops. Even with all the advances made in regulating the industry, exploitation of workers continues. And as at the time of the Triangle Factory, the typical exploited worker is a young woman, often a recent immigrant, and unaware of her rights in the workplace.

But, also as in 1911, employees who organize into effective unions find that they are often able to turn awful working conditions around through negotiations, strikes, and the power of a determined group that knows it is right.

8 One Historic Day: Decades of Changes

Workplace accidents happened every day in the United States in the early 1900s, maiming and killing many workers each year. Thousands of children, often as young as six or seven, went out to work to help their parents provide food and shelter for their families. Activists and union officials, journalists and suffragettes worked hard to raise awareness of the social and political changes that needed to happen to make Americans safer and better off.

But it took the terrible human tragedy of the Triangle Factory fire to truly wake people up. It took the loss of 146 young, innocent lives to cause enough of a public outcry to prompt change.

THE DAY OF THE FIRE

When the fire broke out near closing time that Saturday afternoon, nearly 300 employees of the Triangle Shirtwaist Factory were still at their posts or were cleaning up and preparing to leave. Suddenly the cry went up—"Fire!"—and everyone sprang into action. Some ran for water buckets to try and douse the flames. Others grabbed hoses but quickly discovered there

Suffragettes

The Suffragette movement began in Great Britain in 1832 with the passage of the Reform Act that prohibited women from voting. The word *suffragette* comes from the word *suffrage*, meaning the right to vote in public elections. "Suffragette" generally was applied to women of a radical group within the movement made up of members of the Women's Social and Political Union.

In the United States, most people preferred the less contentious word *suffragist*, which included less radical women as well as men who believed women should be allowed to vote alongside them.

was not enough water pressure; only a trickle came out. Some beat at the flames with nearby material or with their coats.

Within moments, the employees realized that this fire was not like any of the other fires they had had at this factory. Instead, this fire was moving quickly and getting hotter every second. They turned for the exits. Imagine the panic that must have set in when first one door was locked, then the elevator collapsed, then the one available fire escape also collapsed. The ladders from the fire trucks reached to only the sixth or seventh floor, banging uselessly against the side of the building. Large nets and blankets were spread out and held by several onlookers, but the fabric gave way as several girls jumped into them at one time.

Those who knew there was no escape climbed onto windowsills and, as the flames singed skirts and hair, jumped or

To draw attention to their movement, some British suffragettes chained themselves to fences, staged large rallies, and in a few cases, turned violent and set off bombs. Suffragettes in the United States aligned themselves with female garment workers in their struggles to gain better working conditions. The union members in turn joined the ranks of those fighting for the right for women to vote because they realized that they would have a better chance of achieving their goals if they had some say on who would represent them as their elected officials.

Two famous American suffragettes were Elizabeth Cady Stanton and Susan B. Anthony. American women gained the right to vote with the passage of the Nineteenth Amendment in 1920.

fell to their deaths on the sidewalk below. Onlookers gasped and cried and ran about searching for loved ones. The scene is one that survivors and witnesses would never forget and would testify to in graphic details throughout the trial following the event and in many newspaper articles over the coming weeks, months, and years.

Less than half an hour later, it was just about over. Firemen had broken down the locked doors and made their way up the narrow staircases to the ninth floor, where most of the employees had been killed. From outside, fire officials had been hopeful that the number of dead was under 50, but once inside, they found piles of bodies against the locked door, in the elevator shaft, and scattered throughout the hall. A few had died at their workstations, apparently too frightened even to make a move for the exits.

AFTERWARD

Unions quickly joined ranks and, along with organizations such as the Red Cross, sponsored a funeral for the seven women who remained unidentified and also memorialized the dead. A march and rally followed, and a groundswell of unhappiness quickly rose with the current system of laws, regulations, and means of enforcing them.

Within a year, the new Bureau of Fire Prevention consolidated the responsibilities of several agencies and was the first practical, positive effect of the fire. When factory owners

Thousands of mourners gather for the funeral procession of the Triangle Factory fire victims *(above)*. Union members and the Red Cross joined efforts to provide funerals for the unidentified victims. Following a march and rally demanding stricter regulations on workplace safety and workers' rights, the local chapter of the ILGWU met with other organizations to collect money for the victims' families. The owners of the Triangle Waist Factory were later ordered to pay each victim's family $75.

Max Blanck and Isaac Harris were acquitted of manslaughter in December 1911, the public outrage helped to produce other positive effects. People began to believe that more was needed than just laws regulating the number of fire escapes or sprinklers within high-rise buildings. Social changes that were set into motion by the fire and the trial were widespread.

WHAT WAS LEARNED DURING THE TRIAL

During the trial, Fire Chief Edward Croker testified that he could not fight fires in buildings higher than seven stories. He said he had told city officials about this equipment limitation many times. Only the Triangle Company in the top three floors of the building, the eighth, ninth, and tenth floors, was open that day because it was the industry's busy season, and the owners had ordered all employees to work a normal day. So the irony remains that the first seven floors, which could have been saved with the fire trucks' ladders, were unoccupied and undamaged, while the three floors out of reach were crowded and destroyed.

The hallway and stairway that could have provided escape to those people on the ninth floor were inaccessible to most of them because of the locked door. It was customary for only one door to remain open so that factory managers could check the departing workers for stolen material in their pockets or purses. The hallway was lined with bins full of accumulated rags and scraps, creating a hazard, and the one door that was unlocked opened inward, forcing the girls back into the burning room.

A second irony to this sad event was that the great strike of 1910 had started at the Triangle Factory and grown to include 40,000 workers. These striking workers walked picket lines during the bitter cold winter, braving unsympathetic police who were under orders to arrest first and ask questions later. They had to deal with aggressive strikebreakers hired by factory owners and with judges who would rather throw a striking girl into jail for the slightest misdemeanor than allow her to go free and rejoin the picket line.

In spite of the bravery and perseverance of the striking workers, Triangle's owners and those of a few larger factories refused to give in to them. The factory owners formed a group called the Employers' Mutual Protection Association that was something of a union itself. Together they placed ads for strikebreakers and hired thugs to beat picketers. They eventually were able to break the strike.

Outrage and blame surrounding the events of March 25 were directed at the factory's owners. But there were a few who believed, unrealistically, that perhaps the girls themselves were somehow to blame. Perhaps they based their opinions (what we would call "sexist" today) on editorials such as the 1906 *New York Times* editorial that stated, "A nice girl . . . is not thinking about spending her life in commercial employment."

Yet, as pointed out by the national Organization of American Historians on its Web site, millions of so-called nice girls worked very hard in American industry. "Whether it was in textile mills, cigar factories, laundries, or other industries, 'nice girls' endured poverty and the hardship of long hours and dangerous conditions at their workplaces."

When Blanck and Harris were found not guilty, the public was again outraged at what was seen by most people as a miscarriage of justice. As a result, many people were inspired to become activists for workplace reform. Those who were already active advocates became even more ardent in their work to reform the dangers faced by millions of American workers every day.

SOME POSITIVES

As horrible as the fire was, it had some positive effects. It encouraged unions such as the International Ladies' Garment Workers' Union (ILGWU) to organize garment workers and educated workingwomen about the need for suffrage—getting the right to vote. Politicians passed new laws

Frances Perkins *(above)* witnessed the entire Triangle Shirtwaist fire and went on to become the first woman to serve as Secretary of Labor. As a member of President Franklin D. Roosevelt's cabinet, Perkins fought to protect workers by helping form programs like Social Security.

to improve conditions in the workplace, first in New York, and then rapidly across the country. Conditions, for the most part, continued to improve, with new unions forming and becoming ever more organized in the way they conducted their business. The passage of the Nineteenth Amendment in 1920, giving women the right to vote, ushered in ever-increasing awareness for women and the public in general.

Frances Perkins, the first female secretary of labor, appointed by Franklin D. Roosevelt, and a witness to the Triangle fire, also was a member of the Factory Investigating

Commission that suggested stronger safety measures be implemented. She appeared at an event commemorating the 50th anniversary of the event in 1961. She spoke of her experiences on March 25 and how that day woke up society to the depth of the problems that had existed in the factory system, and about the laws passed in its aftermath. She said, "They did not die in vain and we will never forget them."

Chronology

| 1790s | The first trade unions are formed in the United States, including Philadelphia shoemakers, Boston carpenters, and New York printers. The first strike takes place in 1799 by the shoemakers' union in Philadelphia. |

| 1813–1824 | Textile assembly line factories are built in Waltham and Lowell, Massachusetts. They turn raw cotton into cloth. |

| 1820s | The first industrial unions are formed, composed of workers within the same type of industries. |

| 1830–1860 | Immigration swells to nearly 5 million people. |

| 1831 | The first all-female strike is held in 1831 by members of the United Tailoresses Society of New York. The strike involves about 1,600 women and lasts for about five weeks. |

| 1833 | The first tenement building is built on Water Street in lower Manhattan. The cramped apartment becomes the standard for immigrants in the city. |

| 1834 | The Lowell, Massachusetts, Female Labor Reform Association, representing female garment workers in the Lowell mills, strikes and wins their request for a 10-hour workday—a major victory. |

| 1864 | The Working Women's Union is formed. Its motto is "Union, hand in hand." |

| 1866 | The National Labor Union is formed. Its members want to establish an eight-hour |

workday, stop employers from bringing in prison inmates to work for free, and restrict immigration. It also urges sewing women to demand equal pay for equal work.

1886   The American Federation of Labor is formed, composed of small unions of skilled workers.

1887   President Ulysses S. Grant signs the National Eight-Hour Law giving government workers the same amount of pay for working an eight-hour day. This law encourages private-industry unions to push for fewer working hours.

1900   The International Ladies' Garment Workers' Union is formed. Child labor is still legal in

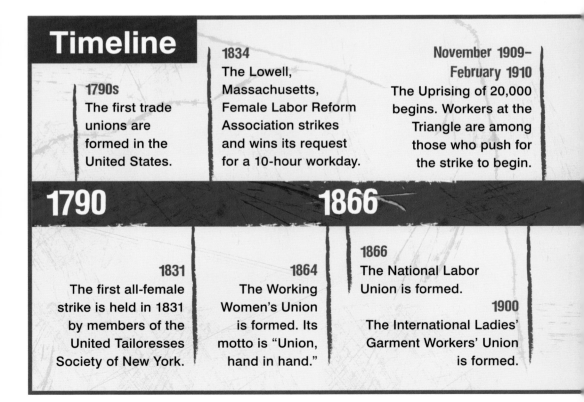

Timeline

1790s
The first trade unions are formed in the United States.

1834
The Lowell, Massachusetts, Female Labor Reform Association strikes and wins its request for a 10-hour workday.

November 1909– February 1910
The Uprising of 20,000 begins. Workers at the Triangle are among those who push for the strike to begin.

1790   1866

1831
The first all-female strike is held in 1831 by members of the United Tailoresses Society of New York.

1864
The Working Women's Union is formed. Its motto is "Union, hand in hand."

1866
The National Labor Union is formed.

1900
The International Ladies' Garment Workers' Union is formed.

many industries, including mining, farming, and the garment trade: About 250,000 children under the age of 15 work legally. Russian immigrants Max Blanck and Isaac Harris start a small business called the Triangle Waist Company.

1903   The Women's Trade Union League becomes a prime supporter of female garment workers.

1909   **November–February 1910:** The Uprising of 20,000 begins. Workers at the Triangle are among those who push for the strike to begin.

1911   Child labor reform laws have been passed nationwide, however, children still work

---

Saturday, March 25, 1911
146 workers are killed in a fire at the Triangle Factory.

April 5, 1911
A march is held to honor those who died in the tragedy. Hundreds of thousands turn out for the tribute, which also becomes a protest against unsafe working conditions.

August 18, 1920
The Nineteenth Amendment to the U.S. Constitution is passed, giving women the right to vote.

1911   1970

June 30, 1911
The Factory Investigating Commission is formed by the New York state legislature.

December 1911
The Triangle Factory owners, Blanck and Harris, go on trial for manslaughter.

December 29, 1970
U.S. president Richard Nixon signs the Occupational Safety and Health Act, which regulates all workplace health and safety issues.

illegally. About 7.5 million women work. In the cities, they are mainly seamstresses in sweatshops or they do piecework at home.

Saturday, March 25: 146 workers are killed in a fire at the Triangle Factory in New York's Lower East Side. This tragedy is still one of the worst workplace disasters in the country.

April: The Committee on Safety forms, joining the WTUL and ILGWU in pushing for investigations into the fire and workplace safety in general.

April 5: A march is held to honor those who died in the tragedy. Hundreds of thousands turn out for the tribute, which also becomes a protest against unsafe working conditions.

June 30: The Factory Investigating Commission is formed by the New York state legislature. The investigation is the most comprehensive look into workplace conditions ever done and continues through 1912. Thirteen new laws regulating fire safety, sanitation, ventilation, and machinery safety are passed directly from the efforts of this group.

December: The Triangle Factory owners, Blanck and Harris, go on trial for manslaughter. They are acquitted in spite of the testimony of 150 witnesses against them.

1912

An investigation by the National Child Labor Committee in New York State reveals that 251 children under age 16 are working, out of 181 families surveyed.

1920   **August 18:**   The Nineteenth Amendment to the U.S. Constitution is passed, giving women the right to vote.

1970   **December 29:** U.S. president Richard Nixon signs the Occupational Safety and Health Act, which regulates all workplace health and safety issues.

2003   The Joseph J. Asch Building, the site of the Triangle Factory, is designated a New York City landmark.

Glossary

blacklist A list that was circulated among business owners naming employees who were considered troublemakers. Often, it took very little for a name to end up on such a list, and once it did, the worker might never find work again.

collective bargaining A process of negotiation between a group of employees and their employer that usually results in a written contract of agreement on issues such as hours, pay, and other workplace conditions.

dysentery An infectious disease caused by bacteria present in unsanitary conditions and marked by fever and severe diarrhea.

heirloom Something passed down within one family for generations. These objects may not have much financial value but often have great sentimental value for the memories they hold.

immigrant A person who comes to live in a new country, one in which he or she was not born.

industrialization A process of changing from work that is done mostly in the home or small group settings to one in which work is done in large settings, such as factories. As a country industrializes, it goes through social and economic changes, as more people move to urban areas, work more closely together, earn (generally) more money, and move away from the natural environment.

industrial unions These groups were organized by men who worked in the same type of industry regardless of the type of job they held within that industry.

International Ladies' Garment Workers' Union (ILGWU) Formed in 1900, this union included women who made shirtwaists, hats, children's clothes, and other items. This union remains active and well known today.

ironclad A document that some factory owners forced employees to sign. This contract promised the employee would not join a union. The worker could be fired if he or she went ahead and joined a union anyway.

mill girls Young women and girls who worked in the garment factories, or mills.

muckrakers A term coined by U.S. president Theodore Roosevelt for journalists and authors during the first decade of the twentieth century who wrote about social issues such as child labor, crime, and government corruption in order to bring about reform.

mutual aid society A group or association formed to provide support—financial and emotional—to others, usually of the same ethnic, cultural, or religious background.

New York's Lower East Side The area of Manhattan bounded by Fourth Street on the north, Catherine Street on the south, Broadway on the west, and the East River on the east. This section of the city was where the Triangle Factory building was located and where most Jewish immigrants settled at the beginning of the twentieth century.

Old World This phrase refers to the Eastern Hemisphere, Europe, Asia, and Africa—parts of the world that were known before Christopher Columbus sailed for the "New World," or parts unknown. It also referred to the countries in which immigrants lived before moving to America.

piecework Women and girls (sometimes children) who worked on a specific piece of a garment were called pieceworkers. So, one woman might sew collars onto blouses, while another sewed on the buttons, and still another would then hem the bottom. Women who did this piecework were often known as sewing women, and when they did this piecework in their homes, it was also known as homework.

Potato Famine   A terrible period in Irish history, approximately 1846–1849, during which the potato crop failed. Since potatoes were a staple of the Irish diet, many people went hungry and even starved to death. Many immigrated to America during this period.

pushcart peddler   A person who earned a living by selling items out of a cart that was pushed around the neighborhood. Common items for sale included fruit, books, hair ornaments, and small household items.

reformer   Someone who is involved in changing the way things are done. At the time of the Triangle Factory fire, reformers included union organizers fighting for higher pay, fewer hours, and safer working conditions overall for their members.

religious persecution   When members of one faith are treated unfairly or cruelly by people outside of their religion.

scab or strikebreaker   Someone who works or provides workers for an employer while regular employees are on strike.

shirtwaist   A woman's blouse popular in the late 1800s and early 1900s. Shirtwaists had collars and puffy sleeves, buttoned up the back, and were tailored at the waist. They were inexpensive and could be worn for every day or dressier occasions. Women of all classes wore them, usually with long, dark skirts.

slowdown   When workers were dissatisfied with their working conditions, they would sometimes stage a slowdown, meaning they would work very slowly, getting little actual work done.

strike   When a group of employees stop working to protest workplace conditions.

suffragettes Advocates who spoke out for the right of women to vote. Prior to 1920, only men were allowed to vote in any type of election. As more women began to work outside the home, they also began to realize that the poor working conditions they endured would only change once they were able to vote for lawmakers who could vote for such changes. The Nineteenth Amendment was passed in 1920 giving women the right to vote.

sweatshops This term usually defines a workplace with unsanitary and unsafe conditions in which employees must work long hours for low pay. Today, this also refers to workplaces that use child labor.

synagogue A place for Jews to worship and study their religion.

tenement A tall apartment building separated by a narrow alleyway. Each apartment in a tenement was sometimes occupied by many members of one family.

trade union Some of the earliest unions were formed by groups of men who were skilled in the same type of craft or trade. They joined in an attempt to bring safety to dangerous jobs and to regulate hours and wages.

union An organization of workers formed to take complaints or requests to the employer as a group.

wage slaves The term sometimes given to young workers who worked long hours for little pay.

Yiddish The common language of Jews of eastern Europe before World War II, based on German, Hebrew, and Slavic languages. It is written using Hebrew characters and is read from right to left. Jews have spoken Yiddish for more than a thousand years.

Bibliography

BOOKS

Brooks, Thomas R. *Toil and Trouble: A History of American Labor.* New York: Delacorte Press, 1964.

Foner, Philip S. *The AFL in the Progressive Era, 1910–1915.* New York: International Publishers, 1980.

———. *The Policies and Practices of the American Federation of Labor, 1900–1909.* New York: International Publishers, 1964.

Gardner, Joseph L. *Labor on the March: The Story of America's Unions.* New York: American Heritage Publishing Co., 1969.

Goldin, Barbara Diamond. *Fire: The Beginnings of the Labor Movement.* New York: Viking, 1992.

Sherrow, Victoria. *The Triangle Factory Fire.* Brookfield, Conn.: Millbrook Press, 1995.

Von Drehle, David. *Triangle: The Fire That Changed America.* New York: Atlantic Monthly Press, 2003.

WEB SITES

http://www.reviewjournal.com
http://www.law.umkc.edu
http://www.arts.gla.ac.uk/www/ctich/eastside/Preface.html
http://www.tenement.org/
http://www.answers.com
http://memory.loc.gov/learn/features/immig/introduction.html
http://invention.smithsonian.org
http://www.ilr.cornell.edu

Further Reading

Auch, Mary Jane. *Ashes of Roses*. New York: Henry Holt, 2002.

Bader, Bonnie. *East Side Story*. New York: Silver Moon Press, 1993.

Diner, Hasie R. *Lower East Side Memories: A Jewish Place in America*. Princeton, N.J.: Princeton University Press, 2000.

Gardner, Joseph L. *Labor on the March: The Story of America's Unions*. New York: American Heritage Publishing Co., 1969.

Gunderson, Jessica. *The Triangle Shirtwaist Factory Fire*. Mankota, Minn.: Capstone Press, 2006.

Hurwitz, Johanna. *Dear Emma*. New York: HarperCollins, 2002.

McNeese, Tim. *The Progressive Movement*. New York: Chelsea House, 2007.

Picture Credits

Index

About the Author

BRENDA LANGE has been a journalist, author, and public relations professional for 20 years. During that time, she has written for newspapers, magazines, and trade publications, and performed public relations functions for a diverse clientele. *The Triangle Shirtwaist Factory Fire* is her fifth book for Chelsea House. She also has revised two other titles. Brenda is a member of the American Society of Journalists and Authors (ASJA) and the Society of Professional Journalists (SPJ) and lives and works in Doylestown, Pennsylvania. www.brendalange.com